Country Library

THE ENGLISH PATH

Before this century most country dwellers made their short journeys on foot. To them paths were as important as roads as a means of communication. Footpaths and bridlepaths led from village to village, to hamlet or outlying farm, to the church, to the inn, to the mill, to a spring, to any place where people regularly went. Yet, unlike roads, their history remains largely unwritten.

In *The English Path*, Kim Taplin sets out to show us both something of their history and of the attitudes and 'mental landscapes' which grew from them. The raw materials are the writings of poets and novelists such as Clare, Hardy and Edward Thomas, who knew and loved the English countryside; paths abound in their books, either in descriptions of nature or everyday life or as settings for all kinds of dramatic incidents. The book shows how this network of rights of way through the heart of the countryside has contributed to the special easy intimacy between man and nature which is characteristic of rural England. The illustrations which accompany the text show how English painters of rural subjects have likewise celebrated this common heritage.

There's something rich and joyful to the mind
To view through close and field those crooked shreds
Of footpaths. . . .

JOHN CLARE

A fresh footpath, a fresh flower, a fresh delight.

RICHARD JEFFERIES

The more they are downtrodden the more they flourish.

EDWARD THOMAS

'I don't like roads,' said Morgan Nelly. 'I likes
tow-paths and cattle-droves best.'

JOHN COWPER POWYS

THE ENGLISH PATH

Kim Taplin

THE BOYDELL PRESS

First published in 1979
First published in COUNTRY LIBRARY 1984
by The Boydell Press
PO Box 9, Woodbridge, Suffolk, IP12 3DF

British Library Cataloguing in Publication Data

Taplin, Kim
    The English Path
    1. Trails in literature
    2. English literature – History and criticism
    I. Title   PR 149.T/

ISBN 0 85115 225 2

Printed in Great Britain by
St Edmundsbury Press, Bury St Edmunds, Suffolk

Contents

Preface

MANY people have unwittingly contributed to this book. My mother read George Eliot to me, and *The Golden Treasury*, and planted a love of literature. My father led us out at weekends into the Surrey countryside, "following his nose" or the cryptic directions of "Fieldfare". It was Leslie Stephen's country, always in sight of Leith Hill Tower – although I did not know that then. I would like to thank the committee of the Oxford Fieldpaths Society for leading me quite literally to "fresh woods and pastures new" and for teaching me what I know about the job of preserving real and particular paths. In particular, Rowland Pomfret has been a staunch friend, tirelessly patient in explaining the obvious to me.

I am very grateful to Christopher Hall for his encouragement, for reading a draft, and for his many helpful suggestions. I would like to thank Andrew Motion for introducing me to the poetry of Ivor Gurney and Andrew Young, and Frank Cheeseman, Douglas Gray, Jeremy Hooker, Mary Jacobus, Alison Kemp, Christina Leprevost, Charles Lock, Colin Macleod, David Phillips, Anne Roberts, Walter Taplin and all the many others who have provided references or discussed the book with me.

My daughter Phoebe found some references herself, and she and Nat have walked a long way with me on short legs. My husband Oli has walked and talked with me over many years, and taught me to read maps. Since I had the idea for this book he has encouraged me, read and criticised it, and helped me to get on with it.

I have availed myself largely of the wonderful privilege of reading in the Bodleian Library, and I would like to thank the committee of the English Faculty Library in Oxford for permission to read there also.

Old Whitehill,
November, 1978

List of Illustrations

To Oli, my fellow-farer

1

"Common Thoughts"

BETWEEN the roads, through woods, pastures, parks, arable fields, commons and along waterways there run, all over England, many miles of public paths. Some are much-used and well-defined, and provided with signposts and stiles; but many are all but forgotten, ploughed, obstructed or overgrown, able to be followed only with the help of a map and a desperate determination. At some time nearly all of them have been well-known and well-used. There will be few that someone has not loved, as Robert Southey, though he took little pleasure in walking for its own sake, did his:

> . . . when at the holidays
> Return'd from school, I visited again
> My old accustom'd walks, and found in them
> A joy almost like meeting an old friend.

Before this century all country people except the gentry made their short journeys on foot or on horseback, so that locally paths were as important as roads as a means of communication and in providing mental landscapes. Many people, perhaps the majority, never travelled more than a few miles from home; the paths encompassed their world – a world before television and supermarkets, before so many ugly houses, and, above all, before the motor car. This is not

The Pathway to the Village Church: Thomas Creswick.

the beginning of an orgy of nostalgia. Many things died with the first world war that were obviously better dead; but that is no reason not to preserve or revive the best from the past. We can rediscover something of a slower, quieter, and more rooted existence by seeking out and exploring the familiar paths of the past. Many of the gifts these paths have to give are still there to be enjoyed, and an understanding of their history and original purpose enhances their value.

"Roads, lanes, paths," wrote Geoffrey Grigson, "we use them without reflecting how they are some of man's oldest inscriptions upon the landscape, how they are evidence of the wedding between men and their environment." A good deal has been written about the history of roads, but almost nothing about paths, which led, usually more directly than the roads, from any habitation to anywhere that people habitually went – to other homesteads, hamlets or villages, to churches, schools, inns, mills, barns, quarries, springs, rivers or the coast, heaths and commons and, later, to railways and factories. Up to now Sidney Webb seems to be alone among the historians of roads in taking any interest in footpaths; his book *The Story of the King's Highway* (1906) did devote a few pages to the subject. "We find practically no reference to footpaths (other than footways bordering carriageways) in eighteenth-century highway literature," he wrote, "and the innumerable paths across private land were apparently used by the public without objection." The paths were too slight, too humble and too local to attract the historian: they did not require to be planned, laboured upon, paid for and legislated about nationally, as did the greater highways; nor have the people who chiefly used them been considered suitable subjects for history – until recently. Most "radical" historians have taken an interest in the urban poor, or, if they have discussed the countryside, it has been from an economic rather than a social point of view. Now, however, as interest grows both in local history and in the history of the common man, it will surely not be long before a history of the footpaths is written. The first two chapters of David Sharp's book *Walking in the Country-side* (1978) have made a beginning.

My book is about the place of the footpaths in English literature. English rural writing is full of references to them.

Besides the innumerable paths merely described, or used as settings for conversations (including scores of proposals), they are crowded with incident – escapes, fights, drownings, and even the thrilling denouement of Conan Doyle's *The Hound of the Baskervilles* all occur on footpaths. Poems, novels and even plays unconsciously document their social history, and in understanding a little about that we can appreciate more fully the part they have played in the literary imagination. Village writing – the best of which is Flora Thompson's *Lark Rise to Candleford* – biographies, autobiographies, diaries and letters and many forms of pictorial art present the story of the footpaths.

Besides making plain their practical importance and the extent of their use, we realise when we examine this wealth of material that it is these paths, rather than the roads, that provide the real access to the English countryside. They lead the way to unexpected, hidden landscapes and furnish peaceful places from which to absorb them. It was only by being able to walk them that the writers – and landscape painters – could come to understand that especial harmonious relationship between man and nature that was characteristic of rural England, and could present that intimate, affectionate view of the countryside which we prize, and which has been envied and admired by the natives of other countries as they have envied and admired that countryside itself and its fieldpaths.

Shakespeare and his contemporaries refer to paths, and so do a few seventeenth-century writers; but references are thin in the eighteenth century when most poetry was too polite for them. They appear again in the seventeen-eighties with poets like John Scott of Amwell, of whom his friend John Hoole wrote:

> The greater part of Mr. Scott's poems are turned upon rural imagery; in which it will be found, that his principal merit is novelty in description, and a laudable endeavour to introduce an occasional simplicity of style, perhaps too much rejected by the present fastidious readers of poetry

> . . . *living in the country, and being a close and accurate observer, he painted what he saw* . . .

The italics are mine, to draw attention to phrases which would fit many of the writers I refer to in this book. To us there seems nothing very startling in *The Amoebean Eclogues*; indeed the cries of "O ye shepherds!" and the automatic choice of words like "strayed" for walked and "azure" for blue seem perhaps all too conventional; but the poet of Amwell did enjoy its real paths, and write about them in lines like these:

> In shady lanes the foxglove bells appear,
> And golden spikes the downy mulleins rear;
> The enclosure ditch luxuriant mallows hide;
> And branchy succory crowds the pathway wide.

Though an admirer, John Hoole could not take the shameless modernism that mentioned an "enclosure ditch", masked by mallows though it was. It must have been this kind of thing he had in mind when he referred to the unfortunate admission of "such names and circumstances, as, in my opinion, no versification, however harmonious, can make poetical". In the same way the mud, and brambles, and mere down-to-earth commonness of the paths had made them on the whole unfit subjects for eighteenth-century verse.

Most of the references to footpaths occur in nineteenth- and twentieth-century writing, and the reasons for this are several, but connected. Firstly, rural England in pre-industrial times was largely unenclosed. This meant that access to the countryside was more general, and although there were well-beaten tracks linking regular destinations, one might still wander at will through common or uncultivated land and by a variety of ways along the balks dividing the narrow strips where crops were grown. Secondly, as Raymond Williams has pointed out, pre-industrial literature tended to view the countryside from the standpoint of the wealthy owners of great houses; and these were the few who would have little occasion to use the paths. Thomas Gray's famous poem *Elegy Written in a Country Churchyard* laments the passing of the "village-Hampden" and the "mute inglorious Milton" who never came to fame. It was written at a time when it seemed inconceivable that the "short and simple annals of the poor" could interest a reading public. Since then the lot of the common man has altered beyond recognition, even that of the smaller proportion of men who still work on the land. Very little of our rural writing is actually by agricultural workers, and there is a tendency among well-meaning but misguided critics to overrate what there is; but as democracy advanced and the horizons of the labouring class broadened, so there grew up a kind of writer who was able to observe them as something more human than picturesque puppets or silent servants. Thirdly, to write about nature particularly rather than in generalities, and to write personally and locally – these are unusual before the nineteenth century. Thomson's *Seasons*, a long nature poem which inspired many later poets including Clare, nonetheless never gives the impression of anything so indecorous or confining as walking about on muddy tracks: instead it is a kind of magic carpet tour. The poetry and prose of those who walked in and recorded the countryside in later years might have seemed to Thomson *pedestrian*; but it had its own ways to communicate enthusiasm, even though it had its feet on the ground.

Nearly all those writers who often refer to paths are closely associated with a particular locality; but this does not mean that their ideas are provincial or their significance merely local. Clearly, Thomas Hardy, for example, has achieved recognition as more than just "a Dorset writer". Yet even so, critics who wish to claim place for him among the very highest tend, in attempting to free him from the charge of provincialism, to disparage his value as a rural writer, as though to be "rural" and "major" were incompatible. William Barnes, on the other hand, a near neighbour of Hardy's who wrote his best work in the Dorset dialect, has remained, so to speak, in rural seclusion, visited and loved by few beyond his immediate fellow-country-men. To my mind his work too, though not in any way comparable with Hardy's achievement, is of high literary quality and deserves to be known more widely for its serene and kindly feeling and its lucid, deceptively simple expression. His poetry may be compared to the trees which he so loved: it combines delicate beauties like the leaves with the solid substance of a trunk.

There are a great many second-rung writers who are full of paths: for those who wish to search or who find it agreeable to read romances with a country background Glen Cavaliero's book *The Rural Tradition in the English Novel 1900–1939* provides a bibliography and a pleasant and sure-footed guide through these uncharted forests. In this book I have on the whole kept to writers whom I consider to be of real literary merit, not always wholly "rural" ones – the exceptions being valuable illustrations of particular points.

There are six writers who stand out for their frequent mentions of paths, who attach importance to them for their own sakes and endue them with literary significance. They are John Clare, William Barnes, Thomas Hardy, Richard Jefferies, John Cowper Powys and Edward Thomas. We shall make other acquaintances along the way, but I single out these six for special introduction since they have in common not only their love of walking and the spiritual influence paths had on them but their recognition and acknowledgment of the fact.

The earliest was *John Clare* (1793–1864). He was born in Helpstone, which he described as "a gloomy village in Northamptonshire, on the brink of the Lincolnshire fens". Near there he spent most of his life until he was placed first in a private asylum at Epping and then in the county asylum at Northampton, being subject to fits of depressive madness. An uneducated man, whose parents were illiterate, he was briefly lionized during his lifetime and then neglected again. His happiest hours seem to have been those spent quietly rambling along his native paths, and his best poems record the impressions of those hours in loving, luminous language. The extravagant claims now sometimes made for his poetry, particularly the asylum poetry, do him no service; but increasingly he is being read for his freshness of tone, and his pleasant rural detail. These things we may value in proportion as we value the small things which he describes with such eager love – the birds' nests and eggs, and the wild flowers – things which have little to do with cities and civilisations, but which have often had a soothing and sweetening influence on the human psyche. Scores of his poems refer directly to footpaths, including a sequence of sonnets on the subject, and many others clearly owe much to footpath walks. His skill lay in describing:

> . . . home-bred pictures many a one,
> Green lanes that shut out burning skies
> And old crook'd stiles to rest upon;
> Above them hangs the maple tree,
> Below grass swells a velvet hill,
> And little footpaths sweet to see
> Go seeking sweeter places still.

William Barnes (1800–1886) was a schoolmaster and parson in Dorset, a sane and cultured man who provides a complete contrast to Clare in temperament. He shared with Clare a love of the paths and natural objects, but he loved people more than Clare did. It was the society, rather than the solitude, of the paths that he enjoyed. The fact that much of his poetry is written in Dorset dialect has hindered the wider appreciation he ought to have, but it is in the music and homely significance of that language that his power most appears. If the reader will but try following the green and quiet ways of his verses, he will find that what looked impenetrable is merely a trifle overgrown, and when once set out he will see that the dialect is a slight hindrance soon overcome. In poem after poem he celebrates the paths of his Dorset countryside; he loved his fellow-men, and he loved the well-used paths, because they connected him with his neighbours. He had affection for particular spots, just as Clare had; but he makes more frequent use of place-names, seeing the paths as pleasant to be walked, but also as leading somewhere – Shelvinghay, Pentridge, Woodley, Woodcombe or Beaminster.

Thomas Hardy (1840–1928) covered a wider area of Dorset, and his feeling for roads has often been noted. Nevertheless Dorset paths contribute considerably to the imagery of his poems and are the scene of much of the action in his novels. "In days bygone – Long gone", he wrote:

. . . my father's mother, who is now
Blest with the blest, would take me out to walk.
At such a time I once enquired of her
How looked the spot when first she settled here.
The answer I remember. 'Fifty years
Have passed since then, my child, and change has marked
The face of all things. Yonder garden-plots
And orchards were uncultivated slopes
O'ergrown with bramble bushes, furze and thorn:
That road a narrow path shut in by ferns,
Which, almost trees, obscured the passer-by.'

These lines are from *Domicilium*, probably the earliest poem of Hardy's we have, and they describe his birthplace as it was in about 1800. Happily change has slowed its pace in this particular spot, and, although some unattractive modern building has been permitted, visitors to Higher Bockhampton today will find themselves obliged to park their cars at a short distance and approach the birthplace on foot, along the bridlepath or one of the several footpaths. I should add that Hardy here used the word "road" as he often does to mean only more of a beaten track than that narrow path overhung by bracken. The "roads" of his poems may be set with stiles: to indicate a main road he usually used the term "highway" or "highroad". Paths, then, led out from his first home. He may have walked by footpath to school in Dorchester across Kingston Maurward Eweleaze and the "embowered path beside the Froom" he describes in *Under the Greenwood Tree*. Paths led away across Fordington Great Field from his house Max Gate. He walked alone and in company all over the Wessex country-side that he has made his own. "Mr. Hardy's feeling for roads is a good thing to come across in a poem or a novel", wrote Edward Thomas in *A Literary Pilgrim*. It is. The routes he knew and loved entered deeply into his imagination and gave his writing two things: a satisfying sense of place, coupled with an image of life as a pilgrimage. With the one he might have remained a cosy, "local" writer, and with the other given us a somewhat chilly cliché; but the tension between the two modes of life, the settled and the wander-ing, is in the nature of the human condition, and Hardy's power of conveying that tension is part of his greatness as a writer.

Richard Jefferies (1848–1887) was the son of a small farmer. He ran away from home (and school) at sixteen, but returned to Coate Farm, near Swindon in Wiltshire, and began his writing career by doing descriptive pieces for the local paper. His voracious reading mainly led him to be "literary" with poor results; but his misspent youth in which, as his biographer Edward Thomas tells us, he "hung about on stiles by Maxell and Great Maxell fields, on the footpath to Badbury Lane, or by the brooks, or on the resevoir, or on the downs, and dreamed and thought", served him better. His works have not yet been collected, but his best writing is the undecorated, careful prose of the essays in selections like *The Life of the Fields*, rather than in his fiction. In these his passion for nature finds concentrated, sometimes almost painfully clear, expression, and his love of old paths and tracks is celebrated on almost every page.

John Cowper Powys (1872–1963) wrote vast novels which are just now beginning to receive the recognition they deserve, and the remarkable *Autobiography*. Throughout his long life he was a great walker, and the part played by footpaths in his own psychology and in his writings is considerable. He was the eldest child of a large and interesting family, most of whom enjoyed walking, to which they were introduced by their father, the Reverend Charles Powys. John's *Autobiography*, although entirely reticent about his relationships with the female sex, including his mother, is yet arrestingly frank about minutiae of psychic experience, many important moments of which were connected with paths. He remembers paths from Shirley, Dorchester, Sherborne and Montacute in his childhood, and from Cambridge and Suffolk as a young man. He continued walking out from every town in which he found himself during his wandering thirty years abroad lecturing; but it was a practice learned from English fieldpaths, and it is to these his imagination reverts, and to the English countryside that he turns for the settings of most of his novels.

Lastly, I should mention *Edward Thomas* (1878–1917), one of the poets whose life was tragically cut short by the First World War. His reputation rests chiefly on his small corpus of poems – he only began to write verse in his last two years – and it is clear that but for his untimely death he would have been a major poet. He also wrote a quantity of prose, much of it concerned with the countryside, although he never made a particular locality his own in the way that his admired Richard Jefferies did: Thomas's was a restless, roving spirit. Jefferies had said that country people always walk slowly. Edward Thomas was not really a country person – his wife Helen was able to feel herself a part of country life in a way that he envied but could not share. At any rate, he always walked fast, covering miles quickly with his long strides. D. H. Lawrence once on a twenty-mile walk with him commented "I must teach you to walk like a tramp". Thomas made a hand-to-mouth living as a reviewer and writer, and had to read and write with the same rapidity with which he walked; but the fact that he had to meet deadlines did not prevent his being a first-rate critic. So with the countryside he could, albeit on a quick reading, recognise its qualities. He knew that footpaths were the way in, and was an expert reader of large-scale maps. Helen Thomas tells in her autobiography *As It Was* how when they moved to Hampshire he "of course began exploring the country round, and soon became familiar with the footpaths and byways. We found we were a few miles from Selborne and the place were Cobbett was born". Thomas was on the track of a tradition of rural writing in which his work now takes a high place. One path in particular adds a poignant stroke to his biography; *A Diary in English Woods and Fields* records:

> December 1. Felling the old willows that leant by the Wandle near Wimbledon, once a sweet spot with the green pennon leaves mirrored in the trouty waters. The elms also are going one by one, and the old path blocked.

We know from Helen's book that this was the place they first made love; the path there cannot be trodden twice.

Apart from Edward Thomas, and to some extent Wordsworth, I am not much concerned in this book with the noted literary walkers. Hazlitt, Stevenson, Belloc and the rest all sometimes used footpaths, but the *action* of walking rather than its setting was their primary interest.

Because I have wished to prove from their own pens the importance of footpaths to the imaginations of rural writers, nearly all my quotations are from contexts where a path is specifically indicated. Even so, I gathered far more than I have been able to use. The book is not intended to be an exhaustive survey of footpath references, and the reader will be able to supply others for himself. And further, when once he is aware of the place of paths, he will be able to see for himself that many a passage of descriptive writing, many an incident, will have been drawn from a footpath setting even where the path has no specific mention, even before 1800. The number of anthologies with titles like "The Footpath Way" which turn out to contain little or no direct reference to paths is a tacit acknowledgement of this. And there are individual writers, for example John Masefield or A. E. Housman, who are full of footpath matters though with few specific references.

How do I know when a footpath is mentioned? The most obvious way is from the word "path" itself, in a suitable setting. But I am concerned with public paths, to which everyone has access, and so when Shenstone writes:

Lord of my time, my devious path I bend
Through fringy woodland, or smooth-shaven lawn,
Or pensile grove, or airy cliff ascend,
And hail the scene by Nature's pencil drawn

it does not count. Even without biographical evidence, we can recognise the "devious path" as that of the landscape gardener, guiding Nature's pencil with a little art. Other words, such as "track", "way" and "footway" – always in a suitable context – are also clues, and so is a phrase like "through the fields". Even farm workers used the paths for getting to and from the scene of their labours in a particular field or barn, before the tractor came. Of course there has always been trespassing, and I shall say more about that later on; but most people most of the time used paths, so that a phrase like "through the corn" implies neither vandalism nor poetic licence but the existence of a public right of way. The mention of a footbridge or a plank, or stepping stones, is another good indication, and, of course, a stile. Stiles of all kinds usually suggest a path, since their function is to keep stock in while giving people on foot a means of getting over a fence or through a hedge.

I include bridlepaths. Rural writers seem to walk more often than ride, but the horsepaths provide the same kind of access to the countryside as the footpaths, and people may after all walk as well as ride them. As Cobbett wrote:

. . . my object was, not to see inns and turnpike-roads, but to see the *country*; to see the farmers at *home*, and to see the labourers *in the fields*; and to do this you must go

The Bridlepath at Cookham: Stanley Spencer.

either on foot or on horseback. With a *gig* you cannot get about amongst *bye-lanes* and *across fields*, through bridle-ways and hunting-gates.

I also include some lanes, though this would have meant that walkers and riders sometimes shared them with carts. Many of what were "lanes" in the last century are now roads, and would not now be numbered on the Definitive Maps of the paths. With the coming of the motor car and tarmac hundreds of these narrow ways were buried alive, and walkers and riders deprived not only of peace and fresh air but also of safe passage, since there was hardly ever room for a separate path at the side. E. M. Forster expressed his sense of desolation and outrage at the loss of what had seemed an inalienable right, when he wrote:

The sort of poetry *I* seek resides in objects Man *can't* touch
– like England's grass network of lanes a hundred years
ago, but today he can destroy them.

H. E. Bates identified the coming of the motor car as a bigger
revolution in country life than the enclosures of the commons – significantly, another revolution which had far-
reaching consequences for the footpath system. Of course you
may still legally walk or ride along the tarmacked lanes, but
the pleasure is gone; and so here pedestrians have suffered
a huge, hidden loss. For everything falls back timidly on
either side of a road, while, as Richard Jefferies said, "everything comes pressing lovingly up to the path".

Many a path is public or private by historical accident, yet
once the accident has happened it makes a difference to the
feeling of it. A private path does not contain the possibility
of meetings, nor the sense of the traffic of the "neighbour-
meeting folk", as the sociable William Barnes called them, of
past generations. You might argue, with Meredith's Laetitia
Dale:

> "The parks give us delightful green walks, paths through
> beautiful woods."
> "If there is right of way for the public."
> "There should be," said Miss Dale, wondering, and Clara
> cried: "I chafe at restraint: hedges and palings every-
> where! . . . Of course I can read of this kind of rich English
> country with pleasure in poetry. But it seems to me to
> require poetry. What would you say of human beings
> requiring it?"

It is the paths that human beings have required, and from
which they have made a different kind of poetry and prose
from that which celebrated the prosperity, and privacy, and
privilege of the large country house, that I am concerned
with. The parting advice of Father Gale, at the end of
Scawen Blunt's poem *Worth Forest*, is comic but should be

heeded; along with "Trust in the Lord" and "Take an honest wife", he bids:

> "Guard well thy rights, and cease not to pull down
> All gates that block thy highway to the town,
> Such as that man of Belial, Jacob Sears
> Has set in Crawley Lane these thirty years."

People like Father Gale guarded the one thing they could pass on to the future, and we keep green their memory by caring for our inheritance, and passing it on in our turn.

We cannot all make out of our experience the poetry that will recreate others; but we can all experience the feelings, and we may term them poetic, which recreate ourselves. The feeling that we could "wax lyrical" is open to all of us, and is the common experience of those who walk the field-paths. Clare is the right spokesman here, since he was closer than most poets to the "rude forefathers of the hamlet" mourned in Gray's *Elegy* but did not remain "mute". These lines from his poem *Rural Scenes* sum up what I am trying to say:

> I never saw a man in all my days –
> One whom the calm of quietness pervades –
> Who gave not woods and fields his hearty praise
> And felt a happiness in summer shades.
> There I meet common thoughts, that all may read
> Who love the quiet fields: I note them well,
> Because they give me joy as I proceed,
> And joy renewed when I their beauties tell
> In simple verse and unambitious songs.

What Clare in his modesty calls "common thoughts" are the subject of this book. The word "common" is used ambiguously to mean "shared" or "available to all", as well as the opposite of rare; and it carries too some of the meaning attached to it in the phrase "the common people". A line of Jean Ingelow's – "the common path that common men pursue" – plays on these meanings also. Footpaths were made by common men who were obliged to go afoot; they are open to all, and so shared, as common land is shared. Public footpaths were not made by, or for, the gentry. When in *Pride and Prejudice* Elizabeth Bennett crossed "field after field at a quick pace, jumping over stiles and springing over puddles" she incurred the class scorn of the Misses Bingley for her muddy petticoat and red cheeks, but she claims the approval of Jane Austen and her readers for her independence and indifference to form. Writers who refer to the paths, whatever their own class, are drawing on a common stock of rural experience. They are rural, rather than pastoral, writers; their flora and fauna tend to be local, and accurate. And, too, a knowledge of footpaths cannot be had from a nodding acquaintance with the countryside; it both is and betokens a proper knowledge of country ways.

The highest praise for the footpath system – as distinct from individual paths or localities – has come from Americans in search of the secrets of old England, who have realised that a good many of them lay along the paths, where time seems to pass more slowly, and who moreover have appreciated that this is the way to get to know the countryside.

Washington Irving recognises this in his essay *Rural Life in England*, and he goes on to say that "the stile and footpath leading from the churchyard, across pleasant fields and along shady hedge-rows, according to an immemorial right of way" is one of the "common features of English landscape" which to him "evince a calm and settled security, and hereditary transmission of homebred virtues and local attachments, that speak deeply and touchingly for the moral character of the nation". This is high style for a homely subject, but it contains the truth. John Burroughs was another American who shared his sentiments. He pointed out that the English walked, but not the Americans, and commented:

> . . . a race that neglects or despises this primitive gift, that fears the touch of the soil, that has no footpaths, no community of ownership in the land which they imply, that

warns off the walker as a trespasser, that knows no way but the highway, the carriage-way, that forgets the stile, the footbridge . . . is in a fair way to far more serious degeneracy.

We may at one time have been in danger of such back-sliding, but it now appears from many signs that we are once more becoming aware of our old rights and footways cross-country. Even Henry James in his essay *In Warwickshire* wrote:

> This is especially what takes the fancy of the sympathetic stranger; the level, deep-green meadows, studded here and there with a sturdy oak; the denser grassiness of the footpath, the lily-sheeted pool beside which it passes, the rustic stiles . . .

But one cannot help suspecting that he had "cottoned" to footpaths as proper things for the initiate foreigner to admire, rather than as personal discoveries.

Nathaniel Hawthorne likewise recognised the importance, and the Englishness, of "these by-paths" which:

> . . . admit the wayfarer into the very heart of rural life, and yet do not burden him with a sense of intrusiveness. He has a right to go withersoever they lead him; for with all their shaded privacy they are as much a property of the public as the dusty high-road itself, and by an even older tenure . . . An American farmer would plough across any such path . . . but, here, it is protected by law, and still more by the sacredness that inevitably springs up, in this soil, along the well-defined footprints of the centuries. Old associations are sure to be fragrant herbs in English nostrils, we pull them up as weeds.

Long may we have the wit to identify such herbs and cherish them! Unfortunately, Hawthorne's enthusiastic rhapsody sounds somewhat romantic to the ears of a footpath preservation worker of today. Many an English farmer does not scruple to plough across these paths, for all they are supposedly protected by law; and the sacredness of

The Gleaners at the Stile: Myles Birket Foster.

the old associations of paths is not so readily conceded as it now is for, say, old buildings.

Hawthorne wrote that in 1863. A year later Elihu Burritt, like Hawthorne taking some time off from diplomatic duties, set off to walk from London to John o'Groats. He wanted to see the countryside and understand it. If he went by train or coach, he would miss, he said:

> . . . those generous and delightful institutions of Old England, – the footpaths, that thread pasture, park, and field, seemingly permeating her whole green world with dusky veins for the circulation of human life. To lose all the picturesque lanes and landscapes which these field-paths cross and command, is to lose the great distinctive charm of the country.

Like Hawthorne, he loved the paths for their antiquity and for their contribution to English literature, which latter he saw very clearly:

> The footsteps of a dozen generations have given them the force and sanctity of a popular right . . . They run through all the prose, poetry, and romance of the rural life of England, permeating the history of green hedges, thatched cottages, morning songs of the lark, moonlight walks, meetings at the style, harvest homes of long ago, and many a romantic narrative of human experience widely read in both hemispheres.

Dedicated to radical causes, Burritt went on to refer to our fieldpath system as "the inheritance of landless millions". The phrase sounds old-fashioned nowadays. We do not need to think in that way of a mass of inarticulate poor: we are not the people, but the public, and we have a voice. And we should not forget that a public path is as surely and legally a part of the king's highway as a motorway – though it is more vulnerable. The quintessential, secluded yet accessible England of Hardy and Constable lies along the footpaths, which have nourished minds whose influence upon our own has been wholesome and sweet. Without them Hardy could not have written, nor Constable painted, what he did. If we value the poets and the painters, we should recognise and cherish the means of access to their subject-matter. Because I love the paths and the imaginative works they have helped to inspire I have put together this book, which traces the relationship of the one to the other.

2

"This Connecting Thread"

OUR present footpath network contains some tracks which go back to prehistoric times, and others from every period in history right down to the few, the very few, that are created today. Most paths are more than a hundred years old. To appreciate what these paths have meant to country people, from the simplest, like Richard Jefferies' cottagers, who only knew that "there always wur a path athwert thuck mead in the ould volk's time", to the most educated, like Andrew Young, who knew that:

> Foot of Briton, formal Roman
> Saxon and Dane and Sussex yeoman

had hollowed the lane before him, we need to realise that the paths which connected people with their neighbours also connected them with their forefathers.

Footpaths are as old as man. Wherever people have regularly gone on foot a trail has appeared, and this trail is the simplest form of man's impression of himself on nature. Animals make trails also, and if you believe that the less impression man makes on nature the better, you can take pleasure in the thought that paths are very natural. The Cornish coast paths struck W. H. Hudson like this:

> The coast road, running from village to village, winding much, now under now over the hills, comes close to some

of the farms and leaves others at a distance; but all these
little human centres are united by a footpath across the
fields. It is very pleasant to follow this slight track, this
connecting thread . . . I recall, too, that some social
rodents . . . have a track of that kind leading from village
to village, worn by the feet of the little animals in visiting
their neighbours. The fields being small you have innumerable stiles to cross . . . but they do not want climbing, as they are nearly all of that Cornish type made with
half a dozen or more large slabs of granite placed gridiron-
wise almost flush with the ground.

Hudson did not mean to be disagreeable in likening human
beings to "social rodents"; on the contrary, he often has a
higher opinion of animals than people, and he finds it
pleasant that the footpaths seem to indicate a merely
animal, an innocent, slight presence. T. H. White was
another writer who preferred animals. His hero Mundy in
Farewell Victoria chose the less frequented footpaths, "the
human rights of way which had been trodden out of the
country by generations, like the paths of rabbits in the dead
bracken. His fathers and the rabbits had been cast from a
common mould, cross-countrymen and dwellers on the
land".

Some of our oldest paths did not arise in the wild animal
manner, by the mere padding of feet. Those which have
survived from very early times are those which were once
deliberately cleared and sometimes metalled as major
thoroughfares, and these have been written about a good
deal. Such are the prehistoric trackways, Pilgrims' and Salt
Ways, Port and Drift Ways, and Roman Roads. Parts of some
of these have become modern roads, but many of the rest
that have survived have done so as humbler rights of way,
and they now provide pleasant walks or rides, full of
memory and legend, but at peace from the twentieth-
century. Shirley Toulson, who has written about the old
drove roads of Wales, is also a poet, and in a recent poem
called *On Peddars' Way* she wrote:

Of pre-Celtic men, who loved
The earth well enough to draw
Over its tractable surface,
Their properly potent lines.

Richard Jefferies describes another such way in *Wild Life in a Southern County*:

A broad green track runs for many a long, long mile across the downs, now following the ridges, now winding past at the foot of a grassy slope, then stretching away through cornfield and fallow. . . . It is distinct from the hard roads of modern construction which at wide intervals cross its course . . . It is not a farm-track: you may walk for twenty miles along it over the hills; neither is it the king's highway . . . The origin of the track goes back into the dimmest antiquity.

In a poem called *The Visions of England* F. T. Palgrave wrote that Rome's hand "with network mile-paths binding plain and hill/Arterialized the land". His image drawn from the circulation of the blood is one which occurs frequently in the writings about the paths.

The use of such antique ways in fiction introduces a sense of history against which the actions of individual human beings at a particular time can be set. This perspective has a different effect according to the writer's temperament. Thomas Hardy repeatedly describes Long-Ash Lane in his novels and tales, dwelling on its altered fortunes since it was a busy Roman road, and the feeling he conveys as his characters make their slow way along it is that the universe has become more implacable, and man's struggles more puny, with the passing years. History gets longer, but individuals do not live longer, nor are they stronger; therefore they seem increasingly to be dwarfed by it. In E. M. Forster's novel *The Longest Journey* Emily chooses an ancient stone circle, approached by a track, to make her revelation about Stephen's birth:

"Here's the path". The bank of grass where he had sat was broken by a gap, through which chariots had entered and farm carts entered now. The track, following the ancient track, led straight through turnips to a similar gap in the second circle, and thence continued, through more turnips, to the central tree.

This particular reminder of the march of time the novelist uses to help us, and the hero, to keep a sense of proportion in assessing his shocks and dilemmas.

To follow, literally, in the footsteps of past generations is to court deep and solemn thoughts which give support against what is ugly and transitory in modern life. As Hilaire Belloc wrote, following the Pilgrims' Way:

> I believed that, as I followed their hesitations at the river-crossings, as I climbed where they had climbed, whence they also had seen a wide plain, as I suffered the fatigue they suffered . . . something of their much keener life would wake again in the blood I drew from them.

Yet even such notable ways as these are vulnerable in a philistine and materialist age, even in a country which believes it values its past. Within a few miles of where I live a Roman Road has been closed as a right of way, and an ancient Port Way "diverted" to make way for a military air base, and in 1977 it was decided to continue to allow motor traffic to mar the surface, the scenery, the peace and the fresh air of the prehistoric Ridgeway, the path Richard Jefferies was describing.

More mysterious even than the recognised ancient ways are the so-called "ley-lines". These were first described by Alfred Watkins in a controversial book *The Old Straight Track*, published in 1925. In it he claimed to have discovered the existence of tracks or leys made by prehistoric people in perfectly straight lines identifiable today by certain clues which he describes in detail – groups of Scotch firs, clefts in hills, monolithic boulders which served as "mark-stones", certain tell-tale place names such as Cold Harbour, and

Christian churches sited in places of earlier religious significance. These tracks made their way over and through improbable obstacles which it would seem more natural to us to try to circumvent; but he argues that the ways of prehistoric people were not our ways. They would, he claims, have been undeterred as children by the fact that the direct route between two points led over a peak or through a pond.

The book is based on some archaeological field-work, and certainly anyone who tries ley-spotting with a large-scale map and ruler finds how astonishingly churches, tumps and Cold Harbours align. But although the book has been recently reprinted and has excited a new wave of interest, it remains not quite respectable. This is partly due to Watkins' belligerent tone towards other archaeologists, and partly to some even less conventional followers of his, who linked leys with flying saucers as the routes of some kind of prehistoric space travel. But although like most aspects of prehistory the leys seem likely to remain speculative, many straight stretches of ancient trackway do exist, and the notion has not been without influence on literature.

An imaginative description of the primal treading out of some such path is given in William Golding's novel *The Spire*:

> . . . a whole procession of travellers with burdens . . . came straight over the nearer ridge from the one so bluely outlined behind it . . . They were saving time, if not labour. In a flash of vision he saw how other feet would cut their track arrowstraight towards the city . . .

Watkins' theory has undergone some kind of metamorphosis here, since these are not prehistoric but mediaeval times. Cold Harbour is mentioned as off, and not on, the straight track. However I include it as an example of the literary influence of the ley-line hypothesis, and the reader who is interested in this topic will find in the novels of John Cowper Powys also that the old ways and landmarks are charged with symbolic force.

Path through a Cornfield: Thomas Churchyard.

Apart from these old roads, the majority of our present paths were made as paths, short, local routes which grew up organically along with the villages themselves. In *The Growth of the Manor* Vinogradoff made this tantalising statement:

> Lastly, there were two subjects, which demanded a good deal of attention and common action, but on which, notwithstanding their importance, we have scarcely time to dwell. I mean the drawing and keeping up of frontiers, and the management of village streets, roads, ways and paths . . . the scattering of the bits of ground to which people had to find access in the course of their farming rendered this last subject especially momentous.

An article by W. O. Ault which deals in detail with some early manor rolls refers to this passage. Some of the rolls he looked at contained complaints over just this kind of right of way; but he comes to the conclusion that:

In general, it would seem that the villagers relied upon ancient custom to assure them of their rights on and upon the common roads, ways, and paths of the village, and that express formulation of these rights in by-laws, at least in the earlier centuries, was not common. In the sixteenth century there are numerous by-laws on this subject.

Whether the paths were normally left uncultivated is in some doubt. It seems likely that in this, as in other social and agricultural matters, the practice differed in different parts of the country according to local custom.

But it was the process of enclosure that gave a firm legal definition to footpaths on more than a local level. The enclosing of the open fields was carried on over several centuries, and a few parts of the country still remain unenclosed today. Thomas Tusser, writing in the sixteenth century, argued in verse in favour of the practice of enclosure, which he saw as conferring general benefits. He makes the old system sound anarchic enough:

> What footpaths are made, and how broad,
> Annoyance too much to be borne,
> With horse and with cattle what road,
> Is made through every man's corn?

It ought, one feels, to have been possible to regulate the number of paths by means of by-laws, or even by force public opinion; and in some areas it certainly must have been managed in a reasonable manner. Enclosure usually meant heavy losses for the people, both of commons and of paths. Many poets lamented the effects of enclosure in their verse, including Oliver Goldsmith in *The Deserted Village*. As Clare wrote in *The Village Minstrel*:

> There once were lanes in nature's freedom dropt,
> There once were paths that every valley wound –
> Inclosure came, and every path was stopt;
> Each tyrant fix'd his sign where paths were found,
> To hint a trespass now who cross'd the ground:

Justice is made to speak as they command;
The high road now must be each stinted bound.

The following statements made by A. W. B. Simpson in his *Introduction to the History of Land Law* (1961) seem at first sight to contradict Clare:

The law relating to easements was greatly developed in the nineteenth century. The progressive urbanization of the country has had a great deal to do with this; so too has the process of enclosure, which made it necessary to define more closely the reciprocal rights and duties of the owners of separate holdings of lands. In the days of the common fields there was for example no need for many of the rights of way which exist today, for the local population could wander where they wished through the unfenced countryside without causing annoyance or injury, and the modern desire for privacy was hardly known.

However, the implication that there are *more* rights of way since enclosure depends on taking the phrase in a specialised legal sense. Clearly, not only was there general access to commons, prior to enclosure, but there were actual paths which were regarded by ancient custom as rights of way even where no written by-laws existed in relation to them; and the law even today says that a path which it can be proved has been used "as of right" for a period of twenty years or more shall be deemed to be public. Paths awarded by the Enclosure Commissioners under the Acts have a pretty well unshakeable status in law; but the price was a high one. As William Barnes wrote, in *The Cost of Improvement*:

Your fathers o'er the downs might rove
Where roadless turf was each man's way;
But you may rarely dare to stray
Beyond the bank'd and narrow drove.
Where they on commons only saw
The worded guidepost's friendly rail,
Now uncouth boards, with threats of law,
Growl, 'No road here, but to the jail.'

John Barrell in a recent book on Clare shows how the effect of enclosure would be to alter the familiar features of a place. "To enclose an open-field parish means in the first place to think of the details of its topography as quite erased from the map. The hostile and mysterious road-system was tamed and made unmysterious by being destroyed . . .". The system, of course, was mysterious only to strangers; to those who knew and loved a few square miles, it was friendly and familiar. ". . . the minute and intricate divisions between lands, strips, furlongs, and fields simply ceased to exist," he goes on:

> . . . Everything about the place, in fact, which made it precisely *this* place, and not that one, was forgotten; the map was drawn blank, except for the village itself, the parish boundary, and perhaps woodland too extensive or too valuable to be cleared, and streams too large to be diverted. The enclosure-comissioner would then mark in the new roads he was to cause to have made to the neighbouring villages, running straight as the contours of the land would allow . . . The effect of enclosure was of course to destroy the sense of place which the old topography expressed, as it destroyed that topography itself.

Such changes would be profoundly disturbing to the natives of the place – most of all to a poet whose inspiration sprang from it. Barrell quotes from Clare's *Journal* in September 1824, where he records:

> Took a walk in the fields saw an old wood stile taken away from a favourite spot which it had occupied all my life the posts were overgrown with ivy and it seemed so akin to nature and the spot where it stood as tho it had taken it on lease for an undisturbed existance it hurt me to see it was gone for my affections claim a friendship with such things . . .

William Barnes expressed his contempt for the "travellen chap", a rootless person who moves too fast to understand the way of life he threatens, and for the neurotically

possessive landowner who threatens the neighbourliness
for which Barnes valued the paths. His tone is not tragic like
Clare's but grimly humorous:

> An' the goocoo wull soon be committed to cage
> Vor a trespass in zomebody's tree.
> Vor 'tis locken up, Thomas, an' blocken up,
> Stranger or brother,
> Men mussen come nigh woone another.

Gerard Manley Hopkins' poem *Binsey Poplars* laments the
brutal destruction of the beloved trees, which changed the
character of a "sweet especial rural scene". Clare and Barnes
suffered a similar but even more complete loss of a dear
landscape, and they speak for all whose daily farings on foot
had given them a sense of place which the enclosures rudely
outraged.

However, the access prior to enclosure was not always
general. Mary Russell Mitford, the author of *Our Village*,
tells us about the situation at Three Mile Cross, near
Reading, in the early nineteenth century:

> We have the good fortune to live in an unenclosed parish,
> and may thank the wise obstinacy of two or three sturdy
> farmers, and the lucky unpopularity of a ranting madcap
> lord of the manor, for preserving the delicious green
> patches, the islets of wilderness amidst cultivation . . .

This sounds excellent, but the situation she describes in the
meadows (as opposed to in completely uncultivated land) is
more worrying:

> There is no path through them, not one . . . They belong to
> a number of small proprietors, who allow each other
> access through their respective grounds, from pure kind-
> ness of neighbourly feeling; a privilege never abused.

One is bound to ask Who is my neighbour? and to wonder
what constituted, or would have constituted, an abuse. The
fact is that permissive access is pleasant for those privileged
at that time – and besides "each other" these "small pro-

prietors" presumably had the *esprit de classe* to include Miss Mitford – but it offers no protection against a change of owner or a change of heart, and it confers no *right* on anyone. The poet William Cowper wrote some agreeable passages in praise of country rambles, and "loved the rural walk": but his chief recreation was on private land – he had a key to Weston Park near Olney – and so I do not use his work in illustration.

Throughout the nineteenth and on into the twentieth century we have writers bearing witness to the regular use of the paths both for business and for pleasure, and also to disputes over their use. The fact that we are hearing about it almost for the first time reflects the emergence of new kinds of writers and writing: but what they describe is a living tradition and not a new phenomenon. At the same time, the question of access first became prominent at a national level, for a variety of related causes which I leave historians to evaluate properly: clearly increases in population, urbanisation, changing attitudes to land ownership, popular rights and reform are involved. Sidney Webb quotes from a letter written in 1809 by H. Clifford to the House of Commons Committee on Broad Wheels and Turnpike Roads:

> . . . any person who may possess only a few acres of land, and finds that the footpath in his neighbourhood either spoils the appearance of his grounds, or deprives them of that privacy he wishes, immediately proceeds barricading the said footpath; puts up a board 'No thoroughfare', 'Shut up by Order of the Justices', 'Shut up by Order of the Commissioners for Enclosing Waste Lands', threatening 'prosecution for trespass as the law directs', and such like intimidations, to the labouring peasant or artificer, who by such artifices are forced out of their road.

This kind of action preceded legislation. By an Act of 1815 two Justices of the Peace were given the power to close a footpath they considered unnecessary. The widespread abuse of this power contributed to the public indignation against the Justices which resulted in the curtailment of their powers by the Reformed Parliament. It was recorded in Hansard in 1831 that one magistrate would commonly say to another, "Come and dine with me: I shall expect you an hour earlier as I want to stop up a footpath."

In Jane Austen's *Emma* Mr. Knightly distinguishes himself as a good landowner and an upright Justice by saying to his brother:

> . . . my idea of moving the path to Langham, of turning it more to the right that it may not cut through the home meadows, I cannot conceive any difficulty. I should not attempt it, if it were to be the means of inconvenience to the Highbury people, but if you call to mind exactly the present line of the path . . . the only way of proving it, however, will be to turn to our maps.

Mr. Knightly introduces the topic to turn the conversation and promote domestic harmony; but his consideration for other people on both counts is intended to command our high approval. The novel was published in 1816, the year following the passing of the iniquitous Act as to Closing Footpaths, and it shows the author to have been more politically aware than is sometimes suggested. In 1829 Wellbeloved in his treatise *On Highways*, found it necessary to remind Justices of their trust:

> In almost every instance, the closing of a public way for the benefit of the proprietor is an absolute gift, without consideration, to an individual out of the possessions of the public. The Legislature has invested Justices with large powers, and they are bound to remember that these powers are to be exercised magisterially. They ought never to grant their assistance as a matter of favour. The Act expressly declares, that the alteration thereby authorized, is to be made only *when the change will be more beneficial to the public.*

As Webb points out, such remarks in a serious legal

textbook amounted to a weighty reproof, and they confirm that attitudes like Mr. Knightly's were unfortunately not usual. The contrariness of Mr. Frankland of Lafter Hall in *The Hound of the Baskervilles* is obviously for humorous effect. He is able to exclaim:

> "It is a great day for me, sir. . . . I have established a right of way through the centre of old Middleton's park, slap across it, sir, within a hundred yards of his own front door. What do you think of that? We'll teach those magnates that they cannot ride roughshod over the rights of the commoners, confound them! And I've closed the wood where the Fernworthy folk used to picnic. These infernal people seem to think that there are no rights of property!"

His attitude is made to look absurd – a comic literary exaggeration – but it is all too typical of the many landowners in public office who apply a double standard.

Under the Highway Bill of 1833, on which the 1835 Act was founded, footpath closures had to come before a jury at Quarter Sessions, and not merely be ratified as they had been in 1815. A further reform was missed by a hair's breadth. "In the Reformed Parliament", Webb tells us:

> so keen was the momentary feeling in favour of preserving footpaths that an amendment came near being carried . . . which would have prohibited . . . ploughing up a public footway. The votes were equal, and the chairman of the committee, George Pryme, proudly relates that he gave his casting vote against the proposed clause . . .

If it were not for George Pryme our footpaths today might be in a better condition, for ploughing is often more effective than barbed wire and notices in discouraging use.

It was from Yorkshire and Lancashire, Webb tells us, that the pressure came for reform on the law of Footpaths, and he mentions a press report of 1832, stating that a petition in favour of the jury clause relating to closures was lying for signature at the warehouse of the Potter Brothers in Manchester. This was the year in which the novelist Elizabeth Gaskell, a friend of William and Mary Howitt, moved to Manchester on getting married; and the wealthy calico printers Edmund and Sidney Potter were close friends of her husband's. It is revealing to read the opening words of her first novel *Mary Barton* with this date in mind:

There are some fields near Manchester, well known to the inhabitants as "Green Heys Fields", through which runs a public footpath to a little village about two miles distant. In spite of these fields being flat, and low, nay, in spite of the want of wood (the great and usual recommendation of level tracts of land), there is a charm about them which strikes even the inhabitant of a mountainous district, who sees and feels the effect of contrast in these commonplace but thoroughly rural fields, with the busy, bustling manufacturing town he left but half an hour ago. Here and there an old black and white farm-house, with its rambling out-buildings, speaks of other times and other occupations than those which now absorb the population of the neighbourhood. Here in their seasons may by seen the country business of haymaking, ploughing, etc., which are such pleasant mysteries for townspeople to watch; and here the artisan, deafened with the noise of tongues and engines, may come to listen awhile to the delicious sounds of rural life: the lowing of cattle, the milkmaid's call, the clatter and cackle of poultry in the old farmyards. You cannot wonder, then, that these fields are popular places of resort at every holiday time; and you would not wonder, if you could see, or I properly describe, the charm of one particular stile, that it should be, on such occasions, a crowded halting-place. Close by it is a deep, clear pond, reflecting in its dark green depths the shadowy trees that bend over it to exclude the sun. The only place where its banks are shelving is on the side next to a rambling farmyard, belonging to one of the old world, gabled, black and white houses I named above, overlooking the field through which the public footpath leads. The porch of this farm-house is covered by a rose-tree, and the little garden surrounding it is crowded with a medley of old-fashioned herbs and flowers planted long ago, when the garden was the only druggist's shop within reach, and allowed to grow in scrambling and wild luxuriance – roses, lavender, sage, balm (for tea), rosemary, pinks and wallflowers, onions and jessamine, in the most republican and indiscriminate order. This farmhouse and garden are within a hundred yards of the stile of which I spoke, leading from the large pasture field into a smaller one, divided by a hedge of hawthorn and blackthorn; and near this stile, on the further side, there runs a tale that primroses may often be found, and occasionally the blue sweet violet on the grassy hedge bank.

Mrs. Gaskell, unlike Jane Austen, is obviously deeply concerned with political questions, although she said of *Mary Barton* "I had no idea it would have proved such a firebrand". The opening of the novel, far from being merely a pleasant purple passage, is a quiet, but earnest and quite deliberate plea for public rights of way, particularly exit paths from the city. Footpaths are scattered through her other novels too, and Mrs. Gaskell's letters show how much she missed the countryside of her childhood on her own account. It was a deprivation she shared with her husband's parishioners, of whose grim lives, as the good wife of a nonconformist minister, she was well aware.

The notion that a path might be used for pleasure as well as for business is not new. Woven into the poetry of William Barnes is a theme of companionable strolls and merry meetings on the paths, and he associates them with holiday and leisure times almost more frequently than with work. Country children played on them, and Sunday walks and evening strolls, particularly as a part of the process of courtship, were an integral part of rural life. But with the Industrial Revolution had come a new kind of attitude to the countryside as an escape, a resting-place, a paradise. This finds its most extreme expression in the works of Dickens.

'A Pleasant Land': Albert Goodwin.

Pre-eminently the novelist of London, Dickens seems to share the attitude of his own Mr. Snagsby:

> . . . in his way, rather a meditative and poetical man; loving to walk in Staple Inn in the summer-time, and to observe how countryfied the sparrows and leaves are

and who having heard of a time

> when Turnstile really was a turnstile, leading slap away into the meadows – gets such a flavour of the country out of this, that he never wants to go there.

When the countryside figures in the novels, it is described in a distinctive tone. Consider this passage from *The Old Curiosity Shop*:

> And thenceforth, every day, and all day long, he waited at her grave, for her. How many pictures of new journeys over pleasant country, of resting-places under the free

broad sky, of rambles in the fields and woods, and paths not often trod . . . rose up before him.

Here the countryside is seen in visionary terms and strongly associated with the idea of death, emphasised by the use of the word "resting-places" following closely on the mention of a grave. The adjective "pleasant" is his stock one. Little Nell's journey in the same book is seen in almost allegorical terms – she actually mentions *Pilgrim's Progress* – as a journey through life to death. As she and her grandfather leave the town the landscape becomes idyllic. They took a path through the wood and

> the further they passed into the deep green shade the more they felt that the tranquil mind of God was there, and shed its peace on them.

Take another example, this one from *Hard Times*. Sissy and Rachael meet on a Sunday to go for a walk in the country beyond Coketown. Sabbath restraint and the contrast with working days gave any Sunday a touch of unreality, but there is more than this behind the entranced description:

> They walked on across the fields and down the shady lanes, sometimes getting over a fragment of fence so rotten that it dropped at a touch of the foot . . . They followed paths and tracks, however slight . . . "It is so still here, Rachael, and the way is so untrodden, that I think we must be the first who have been here all the summer."

There is no sign of life in this countryside, and the detail of the rotten fence reinforces the link with death. Sundays are set apart for God and recreation; they represent the work-people's only escape from their grim enslavement. Their only permanent escape will be into death: the countryside is therefore a prevision of heaven. On this occasion Sissy and Rachael find death – Stephen's death: he has suffered a fatal fall down Old Hell Shaft, from which he is symbolically raised. After that:

They carried him very gently along the fields, and down the lanes, and over the wide landscape; Rachael always holding the hand in hers.

Arthur Clennam's walk to the Meagles' house in *Little Dorrit* produces the same feeling of death-like tranquility, tinged with sadness. Even Walter Gay in *Dombey & Son* proceeds to the fields for an unusually meditative walk. For Dickens the countryside was clean, quiet, good, beautiful *and dead*. Those of his characters who end up living in the country might very well be said to have died happily ever after.

For Dickens the connecting thread seems actually to have broken; the process of urbanisation and industrialisation has gone so far that people are not now any longer joined to their rural past, nor able to draw reviving strength from the countryside. Mrs. Gaskell had lived in the country until her marriage and to her, struggling for air herself as she pitied the working classes, the exit paths from the town still provided a link. The idea that people who were not employed in the countryside might use the paths for re-creation had even appeared in Clare, whom we think of as an utterly rural writer; in his series of sonnets on footpaths we read:

> The pent-up artisan, by pleasure led
> Along their winding ways, right glad employs
> His sabbath leisure in the freshening air;
> The grass, the trees, the sunny sloping sky,
> From his week's prison gives delicious fare.

The nineteenth century saw the formation of the first rambling groups, including the Peak and Northern Footpaths Society. In 1865 was founded the Commons, Open Spaces and Footpaths Preservation Society, whose first Secretary was Leslie Stephen. It arose out of what was known as the Open Space movement, and it aimed to protect public rights of way and rights of access by promoting knowledge of the law. Its good work continues today alongside that of the Ramblers' Association. The story of the early rambling groups and footpath protection societies has been told by Tom Stephenson in *Rucksack*, the journal of the Ramblers' Association, and those who wish can read it there. The Youth Hostels Association and the Holiday Fellowship have both too been concerned with access to the countryside. But the details of these movements are material for another kind of book; all I want to do here is to suggest how early are the origins of what is sometimes thought of as a post-Second World War phenomenon – pressure for access to the countryside from towns.

In the 1880s and '90s that walker and great champion of footpaths Leslie Stephen was leading his stalwart band of intellectuals – known as the Order of the Sunday Tramps – on treks through the Home Counties, the stiff walking stimulating good conversation. Ruskin too, as one might expect, had strong views on the subject of paths. In 1885 he wrote to the *Pall Mall Gazette*:

> Sir – Will you kindly help me to direct general attention to the mischief now continually done by new landowners in the closing of our mountain footpaths? . . . of all the small, mean, and wicked things a landlord can do, shutting his footpath is the nastiest.

In several places in his writings he celebrates the virtues of particular paths, especially those which afford quiet strolls on the outskirts of London, and he deplores their over-use by people who pollute their environment with litter. In *Praeterita* he argues that the mere right of way is not enough; the right is also to a pleasant and commodious walk – a sentiment that Edward Thomas echoed a quarter of a century later.

In the first part of this century a vast number of rural novels were being produced, the public's appetite for such things being then considerable. Books like H. G. Wells's *Mr. Britling Sees it Through*, which presents the values and atmosphere of the pre-war world, typically sets on a footpath the crucial scene in which Mr. Britling consoles Letty in their mutual loss and reaffirms faith in the future of humanity. In the same book the thoughtful American leads the English girl away by stile and path in the correct English rural tradition when he wishes to propose to her. This was published in 1916. Sheila Kaye-Smith's *Little England* (1918) is typical of a particularly prevelant blend of the rural and the patriotic, and she has a character in her first chapter look out from a hillside footpath across the Sussex countryside as far as the coast, seeing the England they are all fighting for. At a stile he pauses to read a letter from his soldier son, and listens to the guns in France. Many who fought in the First World War for their country thought of it in terms of countryside and the values of a rural England, and these pressed for the access which gave them a chance to enjoy it, after the war was over. To some extent the same was true of the Second World War.

In 1946 C. E. M. Joad published a book entitled *The Untutored Townsman's Invasion of the Country*. It is one of several that he wrote which took a shrewd and comprehensive look at the problems involved in access by an exploding population unversed in country ways, and among other things it makes an eloquent plea for the paths. Although it concerns itself in detail with the problems of its time, for instance with recommendations for imminent legislation, it is by no means obsolete. Some schedules of paths had been drawn up under the Rights of Way Act of 1932, but these varied in accuracy and completeness. The National Parks and Access to the Countryside Act of 1949 did not do all that Joad hoped; but it did require County Councils to draw up Definitive Maps, which were to be reviewed every five years. Many authorities have still not completed their *first* quinquennial reviews, and the reorganisation of local government in 1972 has held things up still further. In the case of such as that of West Sussex the map has been made, but numbers of paths have been "rationalised" away: footpath protection societies objected, but such societies cannot cope with collecting and preparing evidence for large numbers of paths at one time, since dedicated though their members often are they are usually working people.

The law relating to footpaths is notoriously complex, and since there are admirable handbooks publised by the Commons Society to assist the layman in coping with its toils I shall not attempt to go into it here. There are several kinds of evidence which can get a path onto the Definitive Map. These are not always easy to produce; however, once a path is on the Map it has the strongest status in law. On these maps, paths are divided into footpaths, bridleways (for riders as well as walkers) and a third category which allows vehicles but is not necessarily maintained to a suitable standard.

Joad felt all the desperation of "a Radical with Tory tastes" when he foretold in his book how the exploding post-war generation would demand access to the countryside. He wanted them to have it, but he feared they would mar it. Raymond Williams would probably not accept the phrase "Tory tastes" for himself; however, call it what you will, when he writes in *The Country and the City*:

> In Britain, identifiably, there is a persistent rural-intellectual radicalism: genuinely and actively hostile to industrialism and capitalism; opposed to commercialism and to the exploitation of environment; attached to country ways and country feelings, the literature and the lore

he is describing the set of values that present one with the dilemma. Many a solidly Tory squire might be found to be opposed and attached in several of these ways, and that is why he might be found cheek-by-jowl with an ardent socialist in an organisation such as the Council for the Protection of Rural England. One may consider that the organisation exists to protect rural England from the public, and the other that it will protect it for the public. Thus only some branches of the CPRE take an interest in rights of way.

Those who enjoy the paths without fighting for them should remember to be grateful to the Commons Society, the Ramblers' Association, a.1d the numerous local groups who do engage in the struggle not only to save individual paths but to press for the right kind of legislation to protect the whole network. Universal cars and television sets took the edge off the open space movement in the fifties and sixties, "I live in the deep country", wrote Herbert Read in *The Contrary Experience*, "yet apart from an occasional game-keeper or a gipsy poaching, I do not remember in the past ten years meeting another walker." Now, however, there are abundant signs of renewed enthusiasm, not least the huge increase in the publication and sales of maps and books of walks.

Footpaths belong to a rural way of life threatened by affluence, and while we must be glad that people are better off, and do not suffer the hardships they once did, we cannot but regret that in the process they forget what was worthwhile in the old way of life. The answer lies in education, but it has to come second. As Hardy wrote in *The Return of the Native*:

> To argue upon the possibility of culture before luxury . . . may be to argue truly, but it is an attempt to disturb a sequence to which humanity has been long accustomed.

Comparative luxury came. Large numbers of people go in for some form of adult education. The trend to invite public participation in such things as the County Structure Plans or new motorway schemes evinces a belief in an educated population. And now that the nation is getting poorer again people are turning back to such activities as home cooking, gardening and walking with an enlightened realisation of the pleasures and benefits of these economies.

As the law stands today, a path may be closed on the grounds that it is "unnecessary". The footpath leading away across three fields behind my house, past a big ash, over a

Old Cottages: Myles Birket Foster.

wooden footbridge and through Peter's Spout Ground where early purple orchids grow, goes from hamlet to village. It is used by a few children going to school, and by any of us who want to go to the village shop or post office, or on a visit, or to a meeting, and the same is still true of many fieldpaths, although it cannot be denied that this kind of use has diminished. However, the cost of petrol has begun to increase it again. Starting out in the other direction are those on pleasure bent; boys going fishing, people wanting to picnic by the river, or simply go for a walk. The purely recreational use of a path is, if you like, a spiritual need. When King Lear's daughters Goneril and Regan tried to deprive him of his followers, they failed to recognise such a thing. Those who want to rationalise away the paths will ask like Goneril and Regan:

> What need you five-and-twenty, ten, or five?
> What need one?

For answer we must cry with Lear:

> O reason not the need! our basest beggars
> Are in the poorest thing superfluous:
> Allow not nature more than nature needs,
> Man's life is cheap as beast's . . .

Footpaths cost absurdly little to maintain compared with the cost of providing other forms of recreation, and much of the time they are left to maintain themselves. They are a cheap luxury, and the pleasure they give is incalculable. The writers from whom I quote in this book plead eloquently for them.

A recent poem by Peter Scupham called *Public Footpath To*, once again uses the image of circulation:

> Such slim capillaries, such seams and crinkles,
> Overflown by clouds, nodded at by thistles,
> Sealed by the impress of lost summer girls
>
> And men whose ways were set by dawn and sunfall,
> Offer a sense of flowers, endurances.

But here the path seems to belong only to the past: modern man is a hesitant intruder. Peter Scupham does not seem to be recalling old associations in order to make us conscious of what we share with the past, but to suggest to us something "lost" and men whose "ways" were not our ways. Proverbs like:

> Essex stiles, Kentish miles, Norfolk wiles, many men beguiles

and children's rimes like:

> Leg over leg as the dog went to Dover,
> When he came to a stile, jump, he went over

show how path and stile were once homely everyday matters: can it be that the "crooked stile" now needs a gloss just as the "crooked sixpence" does? In the first chapter I quoted Hawthorne, likening "old associations" to "fragrant herbs". Fewer people today, even among country-dwellers, can distinguish marjoram, thyme or tansy, and know their uses, than formerly. Once there were myriad varieties of English apple, each with its especial culinary virtues; both the number of varieties and the knowledge of the lore have declined. Likewise, each path is important for its unique character and its contribution to the quality of life. To say that walking should be confined to roads or parks is to ignore any need other than a physical one. Even the exercise area of an enlightened prison may be planted with some token greenery. People have always enjoyed the right to walk through the English countryside, and they have always done so for pleasure as well as for business. In an age of greater material prosperity our spiritual needs increase: we need the quietness and sweet variety the paths can offer.

3

"The Beaten Path"

SOME paths of course were always unfrequented. They may have led to and from isolated houses or barns, or lonely points on river banks or the coast. But many paths now indistinguishable on the ground were once used by numbers of people every day for going to market, to school, to church or to work, and were well-trodden and busy. In this chapter I want to look at the daily traffic of the paths, and to draw their picture as the veins through which human life circulated in the countryside.

One of the delights of Beatrix Potter's classic stories for children is their detail of everyday rural life – the crock of dough, the goffering iron, the hen coop, the potting shed, and the stile. The homely details are not mere background; they are given prominence in the Tales as things of absorbing interest in their own right. In *The Tale of Little Pig Robinson* she describes in detail the route to Stymouth, the market town, noticing not only the scenery, the sounds and the smells, but the very surface of the path itself and the construction of its stiles.

Both the aunts were very, very stout. And the stiles in the neighbourhood of Stymouth are narrow. The footpath from Piggery Porcombe crosses many fields; a red trodden track between short green grass and daisies. And where-

Drawings from *The Tale of Little Pig Robinson:* Beatrix Potter.

ever the footpath crosses over from one field to another field, there is sure to be a stile in the hedge.

So it comes about that Little Pig Robinson has to be sent on a shopping errand for which he is really too young, and which ends in his being kidnapped and taken to sea.

Robinson's route at one point is for a short distance along a road, but pretty soon he leaves it again for another path which gives pedestrians a short cut. Paths like Robinson's were once well-beaten tracks from every village to its nearest market-town; roads accomodated carts and carriages, but were nearly always a longer way round, and those on foot would use the paths, often walking considerable distances. William Howitt describes the institution of market-day as it was in the nineteenth century in a charming and neglected book called *The Rural Life of England* (1838). He describes how early in the day:

The footpaths are filled with a hardy and homely succession of pedestrians, men and women, with their baskets on their arms, containing their butter, eggs, apples, mushrooms, walnuts, nuts, elderberries, blackberries, bundles of herbs, young pigeons, fowls, or whatever happens to be in season. There are boys and girls too, similarly loaded, and also with baskets of birds' nests in spring, cages of young birds and old birds, baskets of tame rabbits, and bunches of cowslips, primroses, and all kinds of flowers and country productions imaginable.

Although he obviously enjoys drawing this picture of the countryside as a horn of plenty, or writing a chapter like *Midsummer in the Fields*, a long rhapsody along meadow paths, he is not blind to poverty, bad weather and exploitation of labour. He and his wife Mary travelled up and down the country and reported very different conditions in different places. That conditions might have varied might seem obvious, but it is often forgotten or glossed over by emotive generalisations about the life of the rural poor in the nineteenth century, whether looking at the bright or the dark side. But despite a degree of objectivity Howitt was "committed". He believed in the benefits of English country life under favourable conditions, its essential wholesomeness in all the connotations of that word, and this makes him a suitable documentary counterpart to the rural poets and novelists, who by and large shared his view.

So, too, did Flora Thompson, writing a century later. Her detailed and unemphatic picture of Lark Rise, the name she gives to the Oxfordshire hamlet of her childhood late in the last century, makes Howitt by comparison appear sentimental and overblown. Yet she, too, despite her personal experience of the life, despite, for instance, having to take her little brother to school by field-path – in this case the longer way – to save him from the rougher children (until she discovered he could fight!), despite this and other rural hardships found much that gave her pleasure both then and in the recollection. Footpaths thread in and out of the story of Lark Rise, as the hamlet women watch for the postman, or the vicar's daughter, to come over the allotment stile, as the paths are used for mushrooming or going to work, for every kind of country business or pleasure. She tells, for example, how she once accompanied her friend Martha, both of them little more than children, to a lonely great house four miles distant to apply for a post in service:

> It was all cross-country going; over fieldpaths and stiles, through spinneys and past villages. . . . The little brother got stones in his shoes, and all their feet felt tired from the rough travelling and the stiff mud which caked their insteps. The mud was a special source of worry to Laura, because she had put on her best boots without asking permission, and knew she would get into trouble about it when she returned.

In her last book *Still Glides the Stream*, the first chapter is called *The Footpath*, and in it the narrator returns to her native village and looks down the path she used to know so well:

> In the days of her childhood the footpath over the meadow had been a hard, well-defined track, much used by men going to their fieldwork, by children going black-berrying, nutting or in search of violets or mushrooms, and, on Sunday evenings, by pairs of sweethearts who preferred the seclusion of the fields and copses beyond to the more public pathways. The footpath had led to a farmhouse and a couple of cottages, and, to the dwellers in these, it had been not only the way to church and school and market, but also the first stage in every journey. It had led to London, to Queensland and Canada, to the Army depot and the troopship. Wedding and christening parties had footed it merrily, and at least one funeral had passed that way.

She uses the footpath as a focal point, and the book takes us back to the writer's childhood and relives some of the many scenes enacted on that path. The book is blurred; it lacks the brilliant sharpness of detail of *Lark Rise*. Flora Thompson had told her tale already, and it is there that it should be read; but I include the quotation from *Still Glides the Stream* because it is so comprehensive a statement of the significance of the path from the farmhouse door by one who knew what she spoke of.

Howitt too has some interesting details of the part played by paths in country life; for instance, his chapter on village children tells how the green lanes would be their play-grounds as well as the scene of their earliest employment, as small children were sent out there to mind big babies, to open and shut lonely gates for horseriders (to be sure the stock stayed in and perhaps earn a trifle), or to go on errands, such as taking boots to be repaired. It is clear that Robinson was not the only young person with responsibili-ties, and obviously most of them soon became more compe-tent than he. The picture we have of traffic on the market paths from Howitt, and from Clare, Barnes, Hardy and the rest, is of a steady daily trickle of individual errands, a large concourse of people once a week on market day, and on fair days almost everyone. Hardy's poem *At Casterbridge Fair* shows us the paths leading off in different directions out of the town, and people making their way home by them at the end of a long day:

. . . Away the folk roam
By the 'Hart' and Gray's Bridge into byways and 'drongs',
                                        [narrow ways]
Or across the ridged loam;
The younger ones shrilling the lately heard songs,
The old saying, 'Would we were home'.

That other Dorset poet, the gentle and sociable pastor William Barnes, lover of the paths and their traffic, wrote:

> We souls on foot, with foot-folk meet:
> For we that cannot hope to ride
> For ease or pride, have fellowship.

He enjoyed the way stile-bars were worn glossy with use and the sights the paths afforded of roofs, or of the work of the land being carried on. The paths led to the houses of friends, of girls to be courted, to social meetings such as fairs, or back to a happy home. Always on a footpath, he recalls "How merry young with young folk met in glee"; he passes the "runnen children", the "wold man", the panting maid with her basket and the whistling young men; there are footpath settings for the Wordsworthian encounters with the love child, the child taking her father's lunch to him at work, and the little guide of the blind. Whether he "met unknown, or friend wi' friend", the meetings were welcome; he takes pleasure in the fellowship of the common path.

Sundays and holidays were especially dear to him. The paths were thronged with the workfolk in their brightest clothes, himself among them making his "wanderen way, both to and fro". From one path he has a favourite view across the Blackmore hills, a view enriched by the thought of the friends he will visit there when he has "a holiday to speäre". *Woodley* celebrates a communal outing, a "club-walking" such as Hardy also describes in *Tess*. The club takes a path across "vields where chaps do vur outdo/The Zunday sky, wi' cwoats o'blue" and Barnes enjoys the music as well as the bright spectacle of "poles an' flappen flags". Many people used to walk to the Fancy Fair at Maiden Newton, "An bring, bezides, a biggish knot/Ov all their childern that can trot". "Dear are the paths" leading from nearby villages to the Shillingstone maypole, to Lincham feast, Woodcombe Feast, the feast "by Melhill's brow" or the fair "under Hambledon's side" to all which he celebrates, in different poems, the sociable going and returning. The feasts were yearly reunions with friends and relations at a distance, and if Barnes sees them as occasions of unmitigated pleasure, what crabbed critic shall decry him? Such outings would be planned for and looked forward to; they were high spots in a hard working life unrelieved by packaged entertainment; they required the effort of a long walk: these things made them valued, and it seems probable that despite a gammer or so feeling her age after such a jaunt, or the pain of a young heart jilted, most people

May Day: Randolph Caldecott.

determined to enjoy themselves and did. Easter Monday
was the occasion of a feast in many villages, and May-day
was another time of traditional celebration, when the footpaths would be used by friends and relations thronging in
from the surrounding countryside. A neighbour of mine in
her fifties described how in her teens she regularly walked
with her friends cross-country to the next-door parish on
Easter Monday to such a celebration, so the practice clearly
continued well into the present century. Flora Thompson
records the custom of making up May garlands and touring
with them in procession:

> Sometimes the garlanders would forsake the road for
> stiles and footpaths across buttercup meadows . . . In the
> ordinary course, country children of that day seldom
> went beyond their own parish bounds, and this long trek
> opened up new country to them.

Today's revived May celebrations usually get no further
than the village green, the children having neither the

stamina nor the footwear for more, though they may take their holidays abroad.

Church-going is of course another practice which has declined. Few people go, and often those who do will take their car even when the church is comparatively near their home. At one time Sunday was the focal point of the week and attendance at church the focal point of that day. It meant careful preparation in terms of personal adornment, and the going and returning was a social occasion, a chance to exchange news and develop relationships in an atmosphere of sweet and well-earned idleness.

In *Adam Bede*, the most deeply rural of George Eliot's novels, the Poyser family go by fieldpaths to church, and she describes how "they set Totty on the top of one of the large stones forming the true Loamshire stile, and waited for the loiterers", and how the children see "a perpetual drama going on in the hedgerows". Richard Jefferies' novel *Green Ferne Farm* opens with a scene of Sunday church-going:

> The click of the double wicket-gates – double, to keep other people's sheep out and the rector's sheep in – now began to sound more frequently, as the congregation gathered by twos and threes, coming up the various footpaths that led across the fields.

Even the more genteel might venture to walk the short distance in fine weather: as one of the characters says, "'The Ferne folk be moast sure to come up thuck path this sunny day, 'stead of driving'". Not so the family of the Vicar of Wakefield in Goldsmith's novel; their aspirations to gentility demanded the carriage for going to church so that they may not arrive "all blowzed and red with walking", although the Vicar himself is content to walk. When they fail to arrive, that long-suffering, foolish man is obliged to look for them, and walks back "by the horse-way, which was five miles round, tho' the foot-way was but two".

Edward Thomas described a church as standing "at the hub of many pathways", and one can often observe this effect on a map. Many churches are furnished with several paths, particularly if they serve a number of hamlets as well as the village. Among Barnes's many references to church-paths his poem *The Turnstile* stands out for its use of path and stile as a central and very moving image:

> On Steän-cliff road, 'ithin the drong,
> Up where, as v'ok do pass along,
> The turnen stile, a-païnted white,
> Do sheen by day an' show by night.
> Vor always there, as we did goo
> To church, thik stile did let us drough,
> Wi' spreaden earms that wheel'd to guide
> Us each in turn to tother zide.
> An' vu'st ov all the traïn he took
> My wife, wi' winsome gaït an' look;
> An' then zent on my little maid,
> A-skippen onward, overjaÿ'd
> To reach ageän the pleäce o'pride,
> Her comely mother's left han' zide.
> An' then, a-wheelen roun', he took
> On me, 'ithin his third white nook.
> An' in the fourth, a sheäkèn wild,
> He zent us on our giddy child.
> But eesterday he guided slow
> My downcast Jenny, vull o'woe,
> An' then my little maïd in black,
> A-walken softly on her track;
> An' after he'd a turn'd ageän,
> To let me goo along the leäne,
> He had noo little bwoy to vill
> His last white eärms, an' they stood still.

The slight personification of the turnstile, the image of its friendly embrace – just hinted, and not mawkishly over-done – tells us something about Barnes's attitude to life and death. The little boy had a place in the world which is empty; but instead of feeling bitterness against the accustomed walk for its reminder, Barnes suggests that the inanimate world is affected by his loss also. His daughter Lucy quotes in her biography of him from her brother's notebook, which records Barnes's last visit to his birthplace, in 1883. They went again to all his favourite spots, including the scene of the turnstile, which was by then gone, and its place supplied by bars – a circumstance which must have intensified the poet's sense of the transience of earthly things. Hardy's poem *The Last Signal* tells how he saw a flash of light from Barnes's coffin – "he who in his prime/ Trudg'd so many a time from that gate athwart the land" – as the westering sun caught the brass plate, a signal from across the Dorset landscape they both loved, seen from the path which ran (and still runs) between Max Gate and Came Church, whither Hardy was going to pay his last respects.

"Ding-dong, Ding-dong, Ding-dong" went the bells of the village church in Lark Rise, "and", says Flora Thompson, "when they heard them, the hamlet churchgoers hurried across fields and over stiles, for the Parish Clerk was always threatening to lock the church door when the bells stopped". But neither bell nor clerk spoke out any more when Andrew Young "listened to the lesson" of time and nature in the ruined church at Friston. Priest though he was, he seems to have preferred that lesson to the customary one read from the lectern – certainly his nature poetry is much finer than that of his with more directly religious inspiration. The poem *Friston Church* begins:

> From Friston Church down to the Tiger
> Path through the field runs to and fro,
> Scored with the feet of happy children
> Dead men and women of long ago.

The poet is conscious that the path links us with the past, but offers something to the present also – without it you would miss "the scented orchis" which:

> Shoots from the grass in rosy spire
> Such odour of sanctity was wafted
> Never from stone church with white choir.

Sunday Morning – The Walk from Church: Richard Redgrave.

Probably the most common use of all for the paths was by country workpeople in getting to and from the scene of their labours. The hero of George Eliot's novel *Adam Bede* walks home by footpath from work at the end of the first chapter, going "out of the workyard, and along the highroad" until he presently "struck across the fields". Farm people of course would go anywhere they needed to on their employer's land, but it was easier to use the paths as far as possible. We are not told what George Cooper's employment was, in Miss Mitford's essay *The Shaw*, but this is how she describes the path to it:

> Now we cross the stile, and walk up the fields to the Shaw. How beautifully green this pasture looks! and how finely the evening sun glances between the boles of that clump of trees, beech, and ash, and aspen! and how sweet the hedgerows are with woodbine and wild scabious . . . Here is little Dolly Weston . . . tottering up the path to meet her father. And here is the carroty-polled urchin, George Cooper, returning from work, and singing.

These work-paths usually took the shortest route. Richard Jefferies tells us of the returning female field-workers:

> . . . the wearyful women came homeward from the gleaning and the labour of the field. Their path passed close beneath the great window, and their stooping shadows for a moment shut out the sunshine. Such paths used by the workers, and going right through the grounds of the house, may be found still, where the ancient usage has not yet succumbed to modern privacy, and were once the general custom.

Timothy Tangs, in Hardy's novel *The Woodlanders* was at one point observed "shortening his way homeward by clambering . . . where there was no road, and in opposition to express orders that no path was to be made there"; the shortest path to and from work was something that a countryman who went afoot felt he had a right to.

Clare suggests in his poem *Rural Morning* the reluctance or exhaustion of "Young Hodge the horse-boy" as he "slow climbs the stile" and in *The River Gwash*:

> The weary mower on the meadow path
> With wallets on his shoulders rocks along.

Morning and good weather might make things seem more cheerful. In his *Shepherd's Calendar* he describes how:

> The shepherd goes wi happy stride
> Wi morns long shadow by his side
> Down the dryd lanes neath blooming may
> That once were overshoes in clay.

Paths led to the scene of many different rural occupations; and if honesty compels the rural writers to confess that they were often muddy, or that the returning workpeople were exhausted, yet they tend to sustain the hope, nourished in the case of the 'peasant' poets by their own experience, that such surroundings must be inspiriting despite hard labour, short commons, long hours and lack of education – at least in youth, in summer, and before the day's work. So Bloom-

field describes the boy going to work at dawn in his poem
Spring:

> His sandy way, deep-worn by hasty showers,
> O'er-arch'd with oaks that form'd fantastic bowers . . .
> Gave inspiration . . .

During the last century country people began increasingly
to engage in other than rural occupations, but they frequently still went to work on foot and used the old paths, or
created new ones to get to new places. Hodge's life was
beginning to alter. In Richard Jefferies' *Hodge and his Masters*
we sense too how the face of the countryside is beginning to
alter with it:

> By the footpath, higher up under the close-cropped
> hedge, the yarrow flourished, lifting its white flower be-
> side the trodden soil. The heavy boots of the plate-layers
> walking to and fro to their work on the permanent way
> brushed against it, and crushed the venturous fibres of the
> creeping cinquefoil that stretched into the path.

Anyone treading a path may crush the flowers, and there
seems no reason why a plate-layer's boots should be heavier
than another man's; partly Jefferies is simply making his
usual accurate observation – he noticed the crushed plants
and knew it was the plate-layers who walked that way. But
there is also a suggestion of the iron heel of the industrial
age. For some workers the morning and evening walk was
all they retained of a rural existence, whether it gave merely
fresh air and greenness, or a chance to snare a rabbit. In
Jefferies' *Amateur Poacher* he tells how:

> . . . workmen engaged in the towns, but sleeping several
> miles out in the villages, can keep a register of the slight
> indications they observe morning after morning as they
> cross the fields by footpath to their labour.

People often walked considerable distances: the grandfather
of a friend of mine used to walk six miles before his twelve-
hour day on the railway and after it the six miles back again.

In the novels of D. H. Lawrence the use of footpaths is solidly and carefully observed, with the sureness that can only come from a deep familiarity with a small area of countryside. It is one of the things that identify his writings as belonging to the rural tradition, but the paths serve to demonstrate subtleties of social change within that tradition. In *Sons and Lovers* the path across the fields from the Bottoms to the mine and the station is an important focal point in visualising the setting. The stile is opposite Mrs. Morel's gate; across it she watches the menfolk go and return. It links home and work, the countryside and the industrial world. Mrs. Morel lies in bed hearing the stile gates bang as the colliers go to work. Or she watches her son Paul crossing the field:

> He had a small, compact body that looked full of life. She felt, as she saw him trudging over the field, that where he determined to go he would get. She thought of William. He would have leaped the fence instead of going round to the stile.

So we have Paul in the workaday picture and incidentally a perspective on his nature. For her husband, the mineworker, the path provides a pleasant interlude, a regular and innocent refreshment in a monotonous life:

> He loved the early morning, and the walk across the fields. So he appeared at the pit-top, often with a stalk from the hedge between his teeth, which he chewed all day long to keep his mouth moist, down the mine.

The single lamp-post of the Bottoms is set at the path's end and here the children play in the early dark like moths, disturbed by the appearance of adults from the dark beyond. The book ends with Paul finding his core of self and purpose again after his mother's death. He is on a footpath, in the dark. He is trying to return, as he always has, to his mother.

But yet there was his body, his chest, that leaned against the stile, his hands on the wooden bar. They seemed something.

He realises his independent existence. He turns away from the country towards the town, the umbilical cord cut at last. The symbolism is depressing but seems clear enough: for Lawrence part of the process of growing up was coming to terms with the towns and what they stood for – urban industrial life, without which an intellectually sophisticated cultural life seemed unable any longer to flourish. "Culture has its roots in the deep dung of cash" as he put it, and cash in the twentieth century came from factories.

In *The Rainbow* the stile is again opposite the home gate, and again it provides refreshment for the man of the house:

> He crossed a field that was all yellow with dandelions, on his way to work, and the bath of glowing gold was something at once so sumptuous and so fresh, that he was glad he was away from his shadowy cathedral.

Again, the home-keeping, child-bearing woman never walks the path, though it is an important part of the child's experience:

> At evening, towards six o'clock, Anna very often went across the lane to the stile, and lifted Ursula over into the field, with a 'Go and meet Daddy'. Then Brangwen, coming up the steep round of the hill would see before him on the brow of the path a tiny, tottering, wind-blown little mite . . . When she was a little older, he would see her recklessly climbing over the bars of the stile, in her red pinafore, swinging in peril and tumbling over, picking herself up and flitting towards him.

But the child grows up, and moves townwards, only reverting to country paths for courting, for her encounters with Strebensky.

No reminiscences of a country childhood are complete without a description of the walk to and from school. Alison

Uttley had a particularly alarming walk through a dark wood, and she describes how she used to bribe her school-mates to accompany her part of the way by telling them stories. The occupants of today's school buses may have fewer chillblains than their grandparents, but there is no doubt that they are missing something that the boy in Clare's *Shepherd's Calendar* had who "lolls upon each resting stile" in his way to school:

> And sawns wi many an idle stand
> Wi bookbag swinging in his hand
> And gazes as he passes bye
> On everything that meets his eye.

He sees the "wheat grow green and long", and lambs, and birds, and hears:

> . . . the weeders' toiling song
> Or short note of the changing thrush
> Above him in the white thorn bush
> That o'er the leaning stile bends low
> Loaded wi mockery of snow.

He leans "O'er the brig rail to view the fish" until he is:

> . . . cautioned not to stand so high
> By rosy milkmaid tripping by.

Clare's Returned Soldier saw "the old path where he used to play/At chock and marbles" and has memories from his own childhood of:

> The stiles we rode upon 'all-a-cock-horse',
> The mile-a-minute swee
> On creaking gate.

Robert Louis Stevenson in his *Essays of Travel* represents himself in the approved manner of the serious wayfarer as taking to the footpaths and is surprised to "pass from between the hedgerows and find quite a bustle on the other side, a great coming and going of school-children upon by-

The Milkmaid: Myles Birket Foster.

paths''. One of the paths especially loved by William Barnes was likewise full of life:

> And oh! the path at Shelvinghay;
> An oak-tree here, an oak-tree there;
> With people tripping on their way,
> A comely man, a maiden fair,
> Or children glad to skip and run
> Out home from school with noisy fun.

Kipling understood precisely the nature of path and road, and although by no stretch of the imagination could he be called a radical, his short stories set in the country show that he regarded footpaths as an essential part of the rural way of life, an inalienable right of the people, part of their side of the bargain in a feudal relationship. *An Habitation Enforced* tells how an American couple come to England for a rest cure holiday and stay on to become lords of the manor. George needs to be protected from the busy world (he is a tycoon having a breakdown), and from the farm where they are staying he can even get to the telegraph office in peace:

> "Go to the stile a-top o' the Barn field," said Mary, "and look across Pardons to the next spire. It's directly under. You can't miss it – not if you keep to the footpath."

On the way he and Sophie discover their future home, the deserted Big House. Later, as befits a benevolent land-owner, George gives orders for the foot-bridge to be well repaired: "Make it oak." Kipling makes his attitude quite explicit in the following dialogue between the couple:

> "D'you see that track by Gale Anstey?" They looked down from the edge of the hanger over a cup-like hollow. People by twos and threes in their Sunday best filed slowly along the paths that connected farm to farm.
> "I've never seen so many people on our land before," said Sophie. "Why is it?"
> "To show us we musn't shut up their rights of way."
> "Those cow-tracks we've been using cross-lots?" said Sophie forcibly.
> "Yes. Any one of 'em would cost us two thousand pounds each in legal expenses to close."
> "But we don't want to," she said.
> "The whole community would fight if we did."
> "But it's our land. We can do what we like."
> "It's *not* our land. We've only paid for it. We belong to it, and it belongs to the people – our people, they call 'em."

They learn their duty to "their people" and gradually them-selves settle into a preference for country ways:

> . . . within the three main roads that bounded the blunt triangle of the estate . . . wheels were not used except for farm work. The footpaths served all other purposes. And though at first they had planned improvements, they had soon fallen in with the customs of their hidden kingdom, and moved about the soft-footed ways by woodland, hedgerow and shaw as freely as the rabbits.

The footpaths served all other purposes. In this chapter I have illustrated the chief uses and destinations for errands of the footpaths. William Barnes is probably the chief poet of the paths in their daily, necessary use. To walk the pleasant fieldpaths of his familiar countryside, in comfortable prospect of his home, or with a dear companion, or more gregariously as one of a festive crowd, emerges from Barnes's poetry as his modest and wholesome idea of earthly bliss. His sense of fellowship includes the dead as well as the living as he contemplates:

> The beäten path where vo'k do meet
> A-comen on vrom vur an' near;

and muses:

> How many errands had the veet
> That wore en out along so clear!

4

"Between the Acres of the Rye"

It was a lover and his lass
With a hey and a ho and a hey nonino,
That o'er the green corn-field did pass
In spring time . . .

Between the acres of the rye
With a hey and a ho and a hey nonino
These pretty country-folks would lie
In spring time . . .

THE country custom, with many another now almost entirely eroded, was to carry on one's courting out of doors, along the footpaths and lanes. Sundays and holidays were the usual times, combining leisure and best clothes, and summer evenings after work. "And is it not sweet," demands William Howitt rhetorically, in a chapter entitled *Sunday in the Country*, "where, on some sequestered stile, sit two happy lovers, or where they stray along some twilight path . . .". Flora Thompson tells us of the conventions governing such walks in her part of Oxfordshire in the 1880s, when the couple would:

. . . come out of their respective homes and stroll in the same direction, but not together as yet, for that would have been thought too brazen. As soon as they were out of sight of the windows, they would link up, arm in arm, and saunter along field-paths between the ripening corn, or stand at stiles, whispering and kissing and making love until the dusk deepened and it was time for the girl to go home, for no respectable girl was supposed to be out after ten.

Francis Brett Young's novel *This Little World* (1934) depicts life in the deep country where such customs still continued, and his couples walk slowly home along the paths after evening service; but part of his theme is that the village he describes has to some extent escaped the twentieth century.

To say that a pair were "walking" or "walking out" often carried the sense of an official courtship, and to be seen walking with a girl was considered to be a way of staking a claim and making one's intentions public. Elizabeth and Farfrae in Hardy's *The Mayor of Casterbridge* are spoken of in this sense as walking together, to the consternation of Elizabeth's father Henchard. And in *Jude the Obscure* it is largely through Jude's ignorance of the nice conventions in such matters, and through her feigning an unusual scrupulosity about them, that Arabella ensnares him. Clare wrote:

> The Sunday paths, to pleasant places leading,
> Are graced by couples linking arm in arm.

William Barnes has several poems of courtship expressing quiet pleasure in the company of his love, in lines like:

> An' I do wish a vield a mile,
> As she do sweetly chat an' smile
> Along the drove, or at the stile.

Both his poetry and Clare's afford an agreeable blend of literary convention with a living tradition.

Gentry are not a part of this tradition. They went to church by carriage if it was any distance; if it was near there was often a private path. Their courting was carried on in drawing rooms, or, if out of doors, along the private rides and walks of their parks and gardens. Howitt laments the:

Early Lovers: Frederick Smallfield.

. . . almost total cessation of walking amongst the wealthy. Since the universal use of carriages, for anything I can see, thousands of people might just as well be born without legs at all . . . It is true, as some of them observed, that they walk in their own grounds; but what grounds, however beautiful, can compensate for the fresh feeling of the heath and the down; for the dim solemnity of the wild wood; for open breezy hills, the winding lane, the sight of rustic cottages by the forest side, the tinkle of the herd or the sheep bell, and all the wild sounds and aspects of earth and heaven, to be met with only in the free regions of nature?

Of course there are many degrees of gentility below the county landowners, but their etiquette tended to follow that of the highest class. The effect of the many instances in the novels of better-class courtship on the footpaths is, therefore, either to de-class the lovers, or to convey a suggestion of deliberate Arcadianism, or to enlist our sympathy for the protagonists as true, simple English hearts.

Readers of Jane Austen may remember the "long walk" in *Persuasion*, cross-country by fieldpaths to Winthrop. Henrietta wants to recapture Charles Hayter, and her sister Louisa persuades her to stretch a point socially to do so by making her way on foot to his house; Louisa herself takes the opportunity of rendering her charms more attractive to Captain Wentworth by engaging in the rustic pastime of nutting in a "rough, wild sort of channel" down the centre of a double hedge "quite out of sight and sound" of their companions. In *Wolf Solent* John Cowper Powys has Wolf woo Gerda out of doors because he is wooing her according to the conventions of her class, and not his; nevertheless his own passion, or as he would say, mania, for country rambles is one of the few things he has in common with her.

A great deal of the action in Hardy's novels takes place out of doors, and if out of doors, unless farm workers are actually at work, on a public right of way; and much of the action is concerned in one way or another with courtship. In

Far from the Madding Crowd Gabriel Oak watched Bathsheba's antics on horseback when she was obliged to lie flat because her way "was not a bridlepath – merely a pedestrian's track, and the boughs spread horizontally"; and where Fanny waited for Sergeant Troy:

> The scene was a public path, bordered on the left hand by a river, behind which rose a high wall. On the right was a tract of land, partly meadow and partly moor, reaching, at its remote verge, to a wide undulating upland.

The scene of Bathsheba's first meeting with Troy was "a path through a young plantation of tapering firs" whose dark mysteriousness Hardy describes atmospherically, building up tension by conveying Bathsheba's apprehension as she reaches this spot in her nightly round of the farmstead. For some reason she always fears the path, but reassures herself "by a remembrance that the path was public". Ironically, of course, it is this circumstance that admits the real danger, in the shape of Sergeant Troy. Chapter 29 has the title "Particulars of a Twilight Walk" and describes Bathsheba's meeting with Oak:

> . . . she had gone for a short walk by a path through the neighbouring cornfields . . . Oak . . . took the same path . . . The wheat was now tall, and the path was narrow; thus the way was quite a sunken groove between the embowering thicket on either side.

Gabriel has contrived this encounter in order to escort Bathsheba and give her a word of advice about Troy. But such meetings, though they may be contrived by the characters never seem so by the author, since he is using the paths quite naturally as they were used in the work and recreation of rural life. Angel Clare's courtship of Tess in *Tess of the d'Urbervilles* takes place out of doors in the work-people's manner as:

> . . . they roved along the meads by creeping paths which followed the brinks of trickling tributary brooks, hopping

across by little wooden bridges to the other side, and back again.

The use of the plural suggests the prodigality of the Talbothays countryside, but it also has a lack of precision which is quite unlike the descriptions of paths in *Far from the Madding Crowd*. The impression is one of unreality; Talbothays seems a kind of "lost domain", cut off from the real world. Its paths lead nowhere, existing merely for pleasure, and all too soon Angel and Tess lose them for good.

In Richard Jefferies' novels the test of true worth is a preference for footpaths: Iden, who is something of a touchstone, incurs class scorn for liking to "plant the potatoes and gossip at the stile" and Amaryllis herself elects to go by fieldpath to the fair, thus avoiding the unwelcome company of a suitor equipped with a dog-cart. Jefferies' good lovers of whatever class are always to be found wandering the paths like shepherds and milkmaids. George Eliot's Felix Holt, being a Radical, of course must court Esther in the working men's fashion, and so uses the public paths:

> . . . soon they got into the fields, where there was a right of way towards Little Treby, now following the course of the river, now crossing towards a lane, and now turning into a cart-track through a plantation.

Alas for Hetty Sorel! her seduction by the young squire in *Adam Bede* takes place on the private paths of his own chase, while by contrast Seth and Dinah walk blamelessly "along the hedgerow-path that skirted the pastures and green corn-fields which lay between the village and Hall Farm". Mr. Mybug, the holidaying Bloomsbury intellectual in Stella Gibbons' *Cold Comfort Farm*, naturally turns to the footpaths for rural romance, since bogus rusticity is a prime target of that likeable satire. "Do you cah about walking?" he asks the fastidious heroine Flora.

> Flora was now in a dreadful fix . . . For if she said that she adored walking, Mr. Mybug would drag her for miles in the rain while he talked about sex, and if she said that she

liked it only in moderation, he would make her sit on wet stiles, while he tried to kiss her.

In the E. M. Forster period and bourgeois milieu, just before the First War, the pastoral custom represented a psychological surrender more absolute even than being "engaged". In *A Room with A View* Lucy and Cecil Vyse pause "where a footpath diverged from the highroad", presenting an alternative way back. It is partly her sense of the suburban proprieties that makes her opt for the road, but he urges her:

> "Do you know that you have never once been with me in the fields or the wood since we were engaged?"

Lucy associates him with a room – a drawing room – with no view: his failed ambition to be the natural man for her, and her coming to realise this, are near the centre of their struggle.

Of course, footpaths may be more or less frequented. Lucy's wish to stick to the road was partly a wish to avoid the intimacy of the path. "Lovers' Lanes" all over England attest the human desire to enjoy some of the pleasures of courtship with a degree of privacy. Absolute privacy could not be relied on even then, as one of Barnes's humorous lyrics tells us:

> An' as I walk'd, o'Monday night,
> Drough Meäd wi' Dicky overright
> The Mill, the Miller, at the stile,
> Did stan' an watch us teäke our stroll,
> An' then, a blabben dousty-poll!
> Twold Mother o't.

If you walked arm-in-arm along well-used paths to show off your acquisition, you sought out the more retired ones for kissing and cuddling. Tennyson's:

> Woods where we hid from the wet,
> Stiles where we stayed to be kind

suggest paths of this sort. W. H. Davies enjoyed the

psychic atmosphere of such places, although content with his own company:

> I walk green pathways, where love waits
> To talk in whispers at old gates;
> Past stiles – on which I lean, alone –
> Carved with the names of lovers gone.

J. C. Powys emphasises the eccentricity of the Jobber and Perdita, his hero and heroine in *Weymouth Sands*, by developing their conventional lovers' walk along a cliff path into a frantic dicing with death as they climb down to the erotically carved "clipping stone" and lose their balance while eating sea holly as an aphrodisiac (quite unnecessarily).

Tennyson describes Vivian as behaving, in her wiliness:

> . . . like the tenderest-hearted maid
> That ever bided tryst at village stile.

The tryst is crucial to all lovers; it is a test of earnest on both sides. Shakespeare's Rosalind, an authority on love, makes great play with it, and in Trevor Nunn's production of *As You Like It* (1977) the scene was set for her first tryst with Orlando by a property stile, a very authentic touch. The tryst gives a chance to prove devotion by being early at the appointed spot or to tease, or declare the whole thing off, by turning up late or not at all. It serves a quite different purpose from the girl's being called for at her home. Town lovers arrange such meetings at street corners, or outside certain buildings; country lovers tended to tryst at stiles or at other specified places on footpaths. Writing of "the cottage girl", Jefferies says:

> On Sundays she gladly walks two or more miles across the fields to church, knowing full well that someone will be lounging about a certain stile, or lying on the sward by a gate waiting for her.

> Meet me by the sweetbrier,
> By the molehill swelling there

Waiting: John Everett Millais.

appoints Clare in his most winning manner, and elsewhere he tells a ballad-like tale of a failed tryst. In John Cowper Powys's *Maiden Castle* Thuella bids No-man to a tryst:

"Meet me to-day without fail by the gate a little way up Lovers' Lane where the scummy pond is and that ash you told me about."

Here again, as frequently in Powys, the convention draws attention to the oddity of the characters who make use of it: Thuella and No-man are no ordinary lovers, but indulge in a curious psycho-cerebral flirtation. It is possible that this episode owes something to the meeting between Bathsheba and Sergeant Troy in *Far from the Madding Crowd*, in which Troy indulges in a terrifying and dangerous sword-play directed at her body. A tryst with a similarly unholy flavour, it is not strictly on a footpath; it seems to be common land, that "hollow among the ferns", but it belongs in the same tradition.

Another of the extraordinary Powys family, Llewelyn, wrote a fictional autobiography called *Love and Death*, a title which promises the worst kind of pastoral excesses. It is in fact a rather beautiful story in which he recalls his love affair with the "mediaeval" Dittany Stone in a series of flashbacks while he fights for his life in a crisis of consumption. John always envied his brother his straight-forward, sunny, earthy pleasure in sex; and certainly here, although the couple are both thoughtful, reading mortals, and not mere healthy animals, the physical wooing is charmingly dwelt upon, purged of grossness, but utterly sensual. And it is all done on footpaths in the country manner, from the first encounter, and trysts by a "great white-rinded beech tree", through courtship walks to a closer intimacy. A footpath leads him at last to Dittany's bed. In an essay called *The Haymaking Months* Llewelyn urges lovers to take summer footpath walks in moonlight, dallying along through harvest fields and on footbridges. This kind of romantic sensuality was a philosophy with him: "Moments of this kind should never be held cheap and never be forgotten," he says. "It is not likely that we shall ever know better."

Country matters frequently occurred on country paths – or near them – so much nicer, and often more private, than the succeeding vogue for the backs of cars. D. H. Lawrence's scenes of outdoor consummation are easy to laugh at, but they are highly traditional. Some of the unease may be due to the fact that the lovers are too sophisticated and urban: they are trying to behave like rustic lovers but are too educated. In *Sons and Lovers* when Paul walks with his mother he is serene and secure. They take a seaside holiday and walk the paths to the village and the sea. He teases her for her fear of the plank bridges, acting the protective male as he did on the path to Willey Farm when he found the way, and helped her over the "hateful stiles". His walks with Miriam, on the other hand, move from an ecstatic, almost visionary state of the return from the Easter Monday excursion to Wingfield Manor, when the sun glints on the tiny stones of the path making it appear jewelled, to a tortured condition in which he "walked biting his lips and with clenched fists, going at a great rate. Then, brought up against a stile, he stood for some minutes, and did not move."

Walks with Clara provide him with the sexual experience of which he is frustrated with Miriam. His first real outing with her combines, in time-honoured fashion, a country walk with love-making, but with characteristic Lawrentian absurdities. For a start she jumps from the top of a stile into his arms. Lettie, in *The White Peacock* does this as well. Did Lawrence know some rash girl who insisted on performing this dangerous feat? The description of the wet path and the trees seems accurately observed. One cannot help picturing a lonely figure, notebook in hand, whose imagination warms up a wet walk with the interpolation of a violent love-making. They scramble down a slippery bank to the river and afterwards go out to tea, wondering what the landlady would think if she knew. They would have been covered with leaves and mud – "pools of water . . . the wet, red track already sticky with fallen leaves." Later, when passion begins to cool, they give themselves an extra thrill by choosing a place even nearer to a public path where they can hear people coming and might be discovered. As a result of all this, Clara's husband waylays Paul on his field-path to Daybrook Station, and they fight, by a stile.

In *The Rainbow* Ursula, like many a less intellectual girl, makes use of the public paths with her young man, and sure enough:

> The dark flame leaped up in him. He must give her himself. He must give her the very foundations of himself . . . She started violently, hearing voices. They were near a stile in the dark meadows. 'It's only lovers," he said.

Consummation waits for another occasion when "lingering along, they came to a great oak-tree by the path . . .".

Virginia Woolf's caustic remark that Lawrence's *Nettles* and *Pansies* "read like the sayings that small boys scribble upon stiles to make housemaids jump and titter", is interesting not only for its literary judgment but also for the picture it gives us of the footpaths as settings for graffiti. In *Tess of the d'Urbervilles* gates and stiles are daubed with religious texts, as they are in T. F. Powys's novel *Mr. Tasker's Gods*, which is also set in Dorset. In T. F. Powys the religious texts rub shoulders with earthier legends. Lovers who knew they could not keep tryst left messages or tokens of various kinds. Some carved their loved one's name, as John Eames carved "LILY" on the footbridge in *The Small House at Allington*. Richard Jefferies took an interest in such things, as he did in all footpath matters:

> Sometimes the green lanes are crossed by gates, over which the trees in the hedges each side form a leafy arch. On the top bar of such a gate, rustic lovers often write love messages to their ladies, with a fragment of chalk. Unable from some cause or other to keep the appointed rendez-vous, they leave a few explanatory words in conspicuous

white letters, so that the gate answers the same purpose as the correspondence column in the daily papers. When a gate is not available, they thrust a stick in the ground near the footpath, split the upper end, and place a piece of paper in it with the message.

Barnes's "rustic lover" employed a more primitive device to the same end in the poem called *The String Token*:

> If I do goo on, I can tie up a string
> On a twig o' the woak by the spring.

Alison Uttley writes of posies left at gates and stiles, and this custom goes back a long way, for Fulke Greville's poem tells us how he:

> . . . on Sunday at the Church-stile found,
> A Garland sweet, with true-love knots in flowers.

In the absence of a specific assignation, the footpaths still provided a chance to see and be seen, pursue and be pursued. Clare's paths are full of milkmaids, half-real and half-borrowed from a pastoral tradition. His poem *The Morning Walk* exemplifies his blend of observation with convention, in lines like:

> Where stepping stones stride o'er the brook
> The rosy maid I overtook.

Barnes knew where to find the maidens "in their evenen strolls", and doubtless they strolled with an eye to their admirers. Bloomfield's charming tale of *The Broken Crutch* tells of the simple maid accosted by the squire "upon the footbridge one clear morn". She curtsies "just in his path, no room to sidle round", and so begins their courtship. It ends happily, though not before her father, fearing the worst, has in his rage "bang'd his crutch upon the stile". "It snapt", and Uncle Gilbert is sent with the pieces to sort the squire out, arriving just in time for the wedding. *The Spectator* is witty at the expense of writers who exaggerate female charms, and reports:

Samuel Felt, Haberdasher, wounded in his walk to Islington, by Mrs. Susannah Crosstitch, as she was clambering over a stile.

Whether Mrs. Susannah wounded the unhappy Samuel intentionally will never be known. But in the eighteenth-century it probably took more than ankles to do it. Not so in Dickens' time:

Mr. Pickwick was joking with the young ladies who wouldn't come over the stile while he looked, or who, having pretty feet and unexceptionable ankles, preferred standing on the top-rail for five minutes or so, and declaring that they were too frightened to move . . . Mr. Snodgrass offered Emily far more assistance than the absolute terrors of the stile (although it was full three feet high, and had only a couple of stepping-stones) would seem to require; while one black-eyed young lady in a very nice little pair of boots with fur round the top, was observed to scream very loudly, when Mr. Winkle offered to help her over.

Stiles, gates, stepping stones and rough or wet places all give oppotunities for flirtation, and stiles as well as kissing-gates often commanded a toll. Clare understood the rules of the flirtation game, and the gallantry and coquetry involved. At first, the lover is humble:

> He left the path to let me pass,
> The dropping dews to shun,
> And walked himself among the grass –
> I deemed it kindly done.
> And when his hand was held to me,
> As o'er each stile we went,
> I deemed it rude to say him nay . . .

An accepted lover has rights, however:

> I claimed a kiss at every stile,
> And had her kind replies.

Hardy's poem *The Third Kissing Gate* trifles, in his grim way,

Millfield Lane, Highgate: John Absolon.

with this theme: on reaching the third gate unkissed the girl's figure merges in an embrace with its own shadow, and vanishes.

Hardy often uses the conventions of country courtship in this way. The tragic forces that are at work in his world – I will not debate here the predominance of character, the class struggle or the stars – turn what should be pastoral encounters with happy outcomes awry. Here, for example, are Eustacia and Wildeve in *The Return of the Native*. They are walking across a heath path like a pair of rustic lovers, making the most of the circumstance:

> . . . the irregularities of the path were not visible, and Wildeve occasionally stumbled; whilst Eustacia found it necessary to perform some graceful feats of balancing whenever a small tuft of heather or root of furze protruded itself through the grass of the narrow track and entangled her feet. At these junctures in her progress a hand was invariably stretched forward to steady her.

Such standard Jack and Jill proceedings ought to culminate in a wedding, or at worst a jilting: Hardy metes out death by drowning, one of several incidents in his tales where drowning or near-drowning takes place from a footbridge. The trembling girls whom Angel Clare carries one by one over the flooded lane in *Tess of the d'Urbervilles* all suffer disproportionately for love.

Two poems by William Plomer half follow, half parody Hardy's treatment of the tradition. In one, *A Right of Way 1865*, a disillusioned elderly botanist returns to a courtship path:

> Remarked he, 'A path here
> I seek to discover,
> A right-of-way bang through this garth here,
> Where elsewhiles a lover
> I prinked with a pocket herbarium, necked I and cuddled.'

In another, *The Murder on the Downs*, the lovers set off on a walk in the usual way, only:

'See' said Bert my hand is sweating!
With her lips she touched his palm
As they took the path above the
Valley Farm.

The consummation she and we expect fails to follow:
instead, he murders her.

After all the courtship and as much flirtation as character
and class convention dictates comes, sometimes, a proposal.
Trollope's claim "to me Barset has been a real county" is
substantiated by its footpaths – Eden, Arden, Hobbiton and
the kingdom of the *Faerie Queene* have none. So when John
Eames comes to propose to Lily in *The Last Chronicle of Barset*
he chooses a footpath to do it in. It marks him as a proper
simple man and not a drawing-room waxwork, and has he
not already rescued the Earl from a bull? The lady has many
hesitations in going with him:

> The path proposed lay right across the field into which
> Lily had taken Crosbie when she made her offer to let him
> off from his engagement. Could it be possible that she
> could ever walk there again with another lover?

Eventually, on another occasion, she agrees to. But he still
has to ask the question:

> And in this first field there was more than one path, and
> the children of the village were often there, and it had
> something about it of a public nature. John Eames felt that
> it was by no means a fitting field to say that which he had
> to say . . . Then they had come to the second little gate,
> and beyond that the fields were really fields, and there
> were stiles instead of wicket-gates, and the business of
> the day must be begun.

Lily comes to his aid by chatting:

> "This is the worst stile of all – when Grace and I are here
> together we can never manage it without tearing our-
> selves all to pieces. It is much nicer to have you to help
> me."

So Philip Wakem had proposed to Maggie in *The Mill on the Floss* on the footpath through the Red Deeps, in contrast to the drawing-room Stephen. Arthur Clennam's preference in *Little Dorrit* for walking from London to the Meagles' country cottage marks him out at once in this tradition as having commendable simplicity of taste; and when Minnie comes along the footpath to meet him and give him her final refusal, she is choosing just the right setting. Gabriel Oak, the constant shepherd of *Far from the Madding Crowd*, first proposes to Bathsheba on a footpath; and when Mr. Stockdale, Hardy's Distracted Preacher, wants to propose to Lizzy Newberry he asks her to go for a walk:

> She consented to go; and away they went over a stile, to a shrouded footpath suited for the occasion.

These two wooers of Hardy's are successful in the end.

Nor was Hardy in tragic vein in *Under the Greenwood Tree*. Another of his country courtships to end in what we hope will prove a happy marriage is Dick Dewy's of Fancy Day. After the ceremony comes the rural custom of the wedding walk, although there has been some question whether Fancy is not too high-bred for such a proceeding:

> "And then, of course, when 'tis all over," continued the tranter, "we shall march two and two round the parish."
> "Yes, sure," said Mr. Penny: "two and two: every man hitched up to his woman, 'a b'lieve."
> "I never can make a show of myself in that way!" said Fancy looking at Dick to ascertain if he could.
> "I'm agreed to anything you and the company like, my dear!" said Mr. Richard Dewy heartily.
> "Why we did when we were married, didn't we, Ann?" said the tranter, "and so do everybody, my sonnies." . . .
> "Respectable people don't nowadays," said Fancy. "Still, since poor mother did, I will."

Next she tries to make the bridesmaids walk in pairs, genteelly; but capitulates on that score as well, and "every man to his maid" in the time-honoured manner, they make:

. . . the circuitous return walk through the lanes and fields amid much chattering and laughter, especially when they came to the stiles.

Fancy destroyed an old tradition when she ousted the old choir by her organ-playing; here she rather reluctantly redeems herself.

Many of the Sunday couples out arm in arm would be married ones – until the charm wore off. The Greene King's wife in Thomas Deloney's *The Gentle Craft* complained rather pathetically at being left behind:

. . . it is no small griefe to me, while I sit doating at home, every Sunday and Holy-day, to see how kindely other men walke with their wives, and lovingly beare them company into the fields, that thereby they may have some recreation after their weekes weary toyle.

His churlish riposte is to take her out and walk her off her feet. One of Bloomfield's *Rural Tales* tells of Richard and Kate's Darby and Joan walk on Fair day:

"'Tis forty years, this very day,
Since you and I, old girl, were married!
Look out; the sun shines warm and bright,
The stiles are low, the paths are dry;
I know you cut your corns last night:
Come, be as free from care as I."

As they walk they remember their youthful pranks along the same path. But it was William Barnes above all who loved to celebrate the affectionate strolls of married couples, and who does what it is often said to be impossible to do – communicates the joys of the happily ever after. *Walken Hwome at Night* – "Come this zide, here. I'll be your screen" – and *The Married Peair's Love Walk* – "Come, Etty dear; come out o'door,/An' teake a sweetheart's walk woonce mwore" evoke that dearest companionship. Here is part of his poem *Walk and Talk* where with his usual compactness, seeming simplicity, and understatement, he lets the time of year, the time of day and the situation of the walk all suggest something about the relationship:

> Come up the grove, where softly blow
> The winds, o'er dust, and not with snow,
> A-sighing through the leafless thorn,
> But not o'er flow'rs or eary corn,
> Though still the walk is in the lew [sheltered]
> Beside the gapless hedge of yew,
> And wind-proof ivy, hanging thick
> On oaks beside the tawny rick;
> And let us talk an hour away
> While softly sinks the dying day.
>
> Now few at evening are the sounds
> Of life, on roads or moonpaled grounds;
> So low be here our friendly words
> While stilled around are men and birds,
> Nor startle we the night that dims
> The world to men of weary limbs . . .
>
> For what we tell, and what we own,
> Are ours, and dear to us alone.

5

"Places of No Good Character"

IN the last two chapters I have tried to show how the paths
were used by ordinary country people in pursuit of their
normal business or pleasure. But the paths were also frequented by those whose normal business was outside the
law, or by those who wished for the time being for some
nefarious reason to escape notice. Furthermore a certain
amount of folk lore grew up concerning footpaths, as it did
around virtually any everyday aspect of country life. This lore
associated supernatural beings with certain paths. In this
chapter I look at all the path users who were for one reason
or another beyond the pale of ordinary society.

> One of my worst labours (wrote Clare in his *Autobio-
> graphy*) was a journey to a distant village named Maxey to
> fetch flour once and sometimes twice every week in these
> journeys I had haunted spots to pass and . . . the often-
> heard tales of ghosts and hobgoblins had made me very
> fearful to pass such places at night.

To share his state of mind needs an effort of the imagination. Today (alas) few places even in the country are without
street lighting or a glow in some part of the sky from a
nearby town. Few places are out of the sound of motor
traffic. Few people now walk fieldpaths at night; but in
Howitt's day country people still had occasion to go:

Rustic Civility: William Collins.

. . . to and fro between their homes and the scene of their duties, often through deep and lonesome dells, through deep, o'ershadowed lanes by night; by the cross-road, and over the dreary moor: all places of no good character.

Join the thick darkness before the moon has risen, or the spectral light when she does, and a quiet deep enough to hear cows breathing, with an unsophisticated belief in an afterlife, and it is easier to see how not only a nervous young poet but many less impressionable adult people could be terrified. Later in life Clare claims to have overcome his fear on finding that an individual "ghost" was nothing but a stray foal following him. Curiously, Robert Bloomfield's poem *The Fakenham Ghost* (*Rural Tales*, 1803) tells a story of a similar misapprehension, so it is possible that Clare "borrowed" it.

The lawns were dry in Euston Park;
(Here Truth inspires my tale)
The lonely footpath, still and dark,
Led over hill and dale

the poem runs. An old dame is benighted returning home along it, and filled with folk-lore what is her terror when

. . . a short quick step she hears
Come patting close behind.

Of course people enjoyed playing on their fears, and the often-repeated ghost story was a favourite among fireside winter's tales. Stories frequently attached ghosts and other apparitions not only to the "church-way paths" where Shakespeare's Puck had them glide on Midsummer Night but to many other lanes and paths at any time or season. The characters in Hardy's *The Three Strangers* are apprehensive at the start of the tale because "stories were afloat of a mysterious figure being occasionally seen in some old overgrown trackway or other, remote from turnpike roads". The inhabitants of Cranford had it that there was a ghost "just where Headingley-Causeway branches off from Darkness Lane". In Trollope's *The Last Chronicle of Barset* Lily declares stoutly:

"We are not helpless young ladies in these parts, nor yet timorous . . . We can walk about without being afraid of ghosts, robbers, wild bulls, young men, or gypsies. Come the field path, Grace."

Ghosts thus appear to be quite one of the regular hazards. When William Barnes went with his son in 1883 to re-visit the old haunts around his birthplace, the old man told with a twinkle a tale of his grandfather, who saw a ghost in the dark and gloomy lane leading to the Haunted House "in the form of a fleece of wool". Barnes loved the relish with which the bogey stories would be recounted, and there are splendid comic touches in his *Eclogue: A Ghost*:

JEM: This is a darkish evenen: b'ye afeärd
O'zights? Theäse leän's a-haunted, I've a-heärd.

DICK: . . . clwose ageän the vootpath that do leäd
Vrom higher parish over withy-meäd . . .
Just overright theäse lwonesome spot,
Jack zeed a girt big house-dog wi' a collar,
A-stannen down in thik there hollor.
Lo'k there, he zaid, there's zome girt dog a
prowlen . . .

He takes a stick to the dog, whereupon his arm is super-
naturally afflicted:

'Twer near a month avore he got it well.

To which Jem laconically replies:

That wer vor hetten o'n. He should a-let en
Alwone d'ye zee: 'twer wicked vor to het en.

A curious and uncanonical custom is described by Mary
Webb. It seems that the function of the "sin-eater" at a
funeral was to eat and drink a small offering placed upon
the coffin and to say:

"I give easement and rest now to thee, dear man, that ye
walk not over the fields nor down the by-ways. And for
thy peace I pawn my own soul."

In *Precious Bane*, Gideon has struck a dolorous blow and
killed his own father, and when no sin-eater appears at the
funeral he takes the burden on himself. But his sister detects
the wrong tone for the scapegoat:

. . . when Gideon said, 'Come not down the lanes nor in
our meadows,' I thought he said it like somebody warning off a trespasser.

Witches and fairies seem sometimes to be associated with
footpaths too. Thomas Heywood's Elizabethan play *The
Witches of Lancashire* has witches lurking along footpaths to
catch the hunt. Kipling's well-known poem *The Way*

Through the Woods is in fact attached to a story called *Mark-lake Witches*. More recently, Robert Graves wrote in a poem called *The Two Witches*:

> We sat by the stile of Robin's Lane
> She in a hare and I in a toad.

Fairies, though obviously unconfined in their wanderings, are familiar with the lesser thoroughfares of mortals, which they sometimes use in order to appear to them. The poetry of Walter de la Mare is redolent of green lanes and supernatural presences, making the magical and the homely meet and blend with mutual enrichment. A fairy in *Berries* gives Goodie Jill a tip on where to find blackberries:

> Over the meadows
> To the little green lane,
> That dips to the hay-fields
> Of Farmer Grimes.

Eleanor Farjeon, another Georgian whose blend of rural and supernatural is often similar to de la Mare's, learnt about country lore and footpaths from Edward Thomas. "In Wiltshire . . . we had our first walks together", she wrote in *Edward Thomas, the Last Four Years*, and goes on:

> . . . it was my beginner's experience of large-scale map-walking that took us everywhere except the highroads. In the middle of fields which cows and thawing snow had churned into bog, he paused, clay pipe between his teeth, hazel-stick up-ended under his arm, intent on the map spread open on both hands. Re-folding it, he ploughed across the width of the morass, aware of some completely invisible track.

A few pages later she recalls how a party of friends sallied forth from his cottage and set fire to a notice-board warning off trespassers. "May the fumes suffocate Squire Trevor-Battye, arch-enemy of ancient Rights of Way'", she exclaims. Eleanor Farjeon never approached the stature of her beloved Edward Thomas; and her writing, though pleasant to those who enjoy anything with a Georgian flavour, rarely goes beyond a characteristic mixture of rural life and whimsy. But one of her best children's stories, *Elsie Piddock Skips in her Sleep* tells how "the new lord began to shut up footpaths and destroy rights of way" including one which led over Mount Caburn, where generations of children had always skipped at new moon. As a child, Elsie was a champion skipper, and learned supernatural skills from the fairies in addition. Years later, when the Caburn path is threatened, she returns as the ghost of a little old woman. She persuades the villagers to make a condition with the lord that he will not start to build there until every girl and woman has had a turn and can skip no more. Elsie of course, being a ghost, can skip for ever. I can never read the story without a lump in the throat; it is superbly told, and summarising does it no service. It shows how the path ghost of local lore can suggest to a reflective mind the importance of preserving what has been hallowed by appreciative use.

Both William Barnes and Thomas Hardy were fascinated by folk-lore and folk-tales, however bizarre, for their own sakes; but often such crude material entered fully into their imaginations and was refined. A theme dear to Barnes was respect for the works and ways of our forefathers, and so a legend that a certain old house was haunted leads on to a delicate plea for conservation:

> Their gauzy sheäpes do come an' glide
> By vootways o' their youthvul pride,
> An' while the trees do stan' that grow'd
> Vor them, or walls or steps they know'd
> Do bide in pleäce, they'll always come
> To look upon their e'thly hwome.
> Zoo I would always let alwone
> The girt wold house o' mossy stwone:
> I woulden pull a wing o'n down,
> To meäke their speechless sheädes to frown.

Hardy's poem *Yuletide in a Younger World* laments the passing of what is in effect Barnes's world and the kind of imagination, partly religious, which conjured spirits readily, knew how to celebrate holidays, and treated the past, both old customs and memories, with the respect due to a living thing:

> We had eyes for phantoms then,
> And at bridge or stile
> On Christmas Eve
> Clear beheld those countless ones who had crossed it
> Cross again in file:—
> Such has ceased longwhile!

For Barnes, the much-loved pastor and amateur archaeologist, paths suggest community with those who have gone before as well as with the living; he can accept mortality and the passing of time with thoughtfulness but with equanimity. He can even derive comfort from the fact of landscape outlasting man, because he sees it as made friendly by human associations. For him the paths represent continuity:

> Ah! I do think, as I do tread
> Theäse path, wi' elems overhead,
> A climen slowly up vrom bridge,
> By easy steps to Broadwoak Ridge,
> That all theäse roads that we do bruise . . .
> Be works that we've a-vound a-wrought
> By our vorefathers ceäre an' thought.

Notice, by the way, how the rhythm and syntax suggest the deliberately slow uphill plodding of a practised walker, and so lend solidity to the thought.

Hardy's fervent connecting of people and places is less philosophical. It is more personal, and often bitter. In his landscapes man seems punier, and less effectual. A number of his poems connect footpaths with the phantom presences of friends he has walked them with. *The Head Above the Fog* draws on the country superstition of ghosts on footpaths, but extends it to suggest that a human being can have a permanent psychic effect upon a landscape, an idea which he canvasses frequently. The same is true of *The Dead Quire*, of which J. O. Bailey says:

Though the story is a fantasy, it is realistic in its persons and places. The action takes place in Lower Bock-hampton, along a path beside a branch of the Frome River.

It is in fact the same "embowered path beside the Froom" along which the choir go at the beginning of *Under the Greenwood Tree*. *Old Excursions* gives expression to the softening of mood which time brings to the bereaved. At first he can take no pleasure in revisiting "those haunts we knew":

> But to-night, while walking weary,
> Near me seemed her shade,
> Come as 'twere to upbraid
> This my mood in deeming dreary
> Scenes that used to please;
> And, if she did come to me,
> Still solicitous, there may be
> Good in going to these.
>
> So, I'll care to roam to Ridgeway,
> Cerne, or Sydling Mill,
> Or to Yell'ham Hill,
> Blithely bearing Casterbridge-way
> As we used to do.

Hardy's footpath poems are often an exploration of his attitude to death, and a questioning what part of you survives. In *Her Immortality* he wrote:

> Upon a noon I pilgrimed through
> A pasture, mile by mile.

On this fieldpath he met a ghost whom he longed to join in death; but she begs him to live, for her immortality lasts as long as someone is alive to remember her. I will quote the poem *Paying Calls* in full, because it contains together the ideas of paths, death and old haunts which I have touched on, and its grim twist epitomises Hardy's protest against the fact of death, of places continuing when people are gone:

I went by footpath and by stile
Beyond where bustle ends,
Strayed here a mile and there a mile
And called upon some friends.

On certain ones I had not seen
For years past did I call,
And then on others who had been
The oldest friends of all.

It was the time of midsummer
When they had used to roam;
But now, though tempting was the air,
I found them all at home.

I spoke to one and other of them
By mound and stone and tree
Of things we had done ere days were dim,
But they spoke not to me.

Hardy's own immortality lies in his writings, and through them he still haunts the footways of the Dorset countryside. "My spirit will not haunt the mound/Above my breast", he wrote:

But travel, memory-possessed,
To where my tremulous being found
Life largest, best.

My phantom-footed shape will go
When nightfall grays
Hither and thither along the ways
I and another used to know
In backward days.

And there you'll find me, if a jot
You still should care
For me, and for my curious air;
If otherwise, then I shall not,
For you, be there.

And for those who do care for Hardy, his spirit certainly does speak from every track and tump of that ancient, wind-blown chalk landscape.

More recently Vernon Watkins has touched on the same theme, in the fourth sonnet of *The Pulse and The Shade*. It is the shade who walks the paths, without making any impression on them, in the lines:

> To-day snow covers all the paths and stiles.
> Light through the gateposts, watching the sun rise,
> Stealthily brings, on snow's unprinted aisles,
> That erect figure, ferried back with sighs.

These are the words of one accustomed to walking in the countryside, and the down-to-earth actuality of the landscape makes more real, and at the same time more numinous, the presence of the shade. Watkins' dead, like Hardy's, crowd close upon the living at times.

A few hauntings must be attributable to a specialised and rather macabre use for footpaths: düelling. Since it was against the law, the practice was to choose a recognised but retired spot as the site of an encounter, and such spots seem often to have been approached by footpath. I have found four literary references to such a use – all comic; it is possible they owe something to each other. The earliest is in *The Merry Wives of Windsor* where Sir Hugh Evans waits for Dr. Caius to keep his appointment in the field near Frogmore and eventually sees him coming "over the stile yonder". In Sheridan's *The Rivals* the scene is similarly set. Bob Acres waits in terror in King's Mead Fields for Sir Lucius O'Trigger, and is with difficulty persuaded not to run at the sight of him and his second approaching over the stile. There are also two references in Dickens. Mr. Alexander Trott in *Sketches by Boz* receives his challenge in the following form:

> "Sir. From Great Winglebury Church, a footpath leads through four meadows to a retired spot known to the townspeople as Stiffun's Acre." (Mr. Trott shuddered).
> "I shall be waiting there alone, at twenty minutes before six o'clock tomorrow morning."

And in *Pickwick Papers* Mr. Winkle's affair is similarly arranged:

> "If you will take the trouble to turn into the field which borders the trench, take the foot-path to the left when you arrive at an angle of the fortification, and keep straight on 'till you see me, I will precede you to a secluded place, where the affair can be conducted without fear of interruption."

Part of the comedy arises from the fact that great emphasis is always laid on seclusion, whereas usually one of the parties would much sooner be discovered in time.

These duellists are outlaws only for the time, and for honour's sake. But there are habitual denizens of the paths who are always outlaws, and who scrape a living by more or less dishonest means, avoiding the larger thoroughfares – rogues and vagabonds of all kinds.

Know'st thou the way to Dover?

asks blind Gloucester in *King Lear*.

Both stile and gate, horseway and footpath

answers his son Edgar, in the guise of a Tom o'Bedlam. Consider what his answer tells us. First it speaks of England, and should be garnered up along with Justice Shallow's apples as a rare bit of evidence for Shakespeare the English countryman – a Shakespeare many have airily claimed to recognise but who remains hard to reconstruct from the texts of his plays. It suits our national sentiment for our greatest poet to have had a country childhood, but would we guess it from the plays alone? Still, I am as fond of the picture as anyone, so I offer the line in evidence. Second, it contributes to a central theme of the play. "Unaccomodated man" on his own two legs, the "forked animal", uses footpath and stile. Edgar achieves fitness to rule through suffering the privations of the poorest human beings. Knowing the way on foot to Dover epitomises an understanding of the common man. Edgar's disguise, although taken at first for his own safety, becomes a means to wisdom, to a knowledge most necessary to princes, but not available to travellers along roads accomodated with retinues and fine clothes.

Vagabonds might be villains as well as unfortunates.

> Jog on, jog on the footpath way
> And merrily hent the stile-a

sings Autolycus the coney-catcher in Shakespeare's *The Winter's Tale*. Such as he who lived by cheating and cutting purses, and all vagabonds mad or sane, had good reasons for avoiding the highroad. In Shakespeare's day the punishments for vagrancy were horrific and the asylums, workhouses and gaols of later times were equally to be avoided. On footpaths villains and unfortunates could avoid authority and beg, thieve or simply skulk, in peace. Heywood's Clown in *A Maydenhead Well Lost* says when he plans to turn professional beggar that he has devised prayers to call down on those who give:

> "I have one for the horse-way, another for the foot-way, and a third for the turning-stile."

In *Desperate Remedies* Hardy gives us two kinds of outlaw in the same passage:

> A vagrant first told them that Manston had passed a rick at daybreak, under which this man was lying. They followed the track he pointed out and ultimately came to a stile. On the other side was a heap of half-hardened mud, scraped from the road. On the surface of the heap, where it had been smoothed by the shovel, was distinctly imprinted the form of a man's hand, the buttons of his waistcoat, and his watch-chain showing that he had stumbled in hurrying over the stile, and fallen there . . . They followed on till they reached a ford crossed by stepping-stones – on the further bank were the same footmarks that had shown themselves beside the stile.

Hardy's experiment with the detective story manner sorts

Path by the River Ripley: Arthur D. Peppercorn.

rather oddly with his native stiles and mud. Brother to his "vagrant" is the tramp who is loitering about the stile in Meredith's *The Egoist* and who gives the tip-off that betrays Clara in her attempted escape. In George Eliot's *The Mill on the Floss*, Mr. Tulliver's quarrel with Lawyer Wakem arose over a bridlepath: he reckoned the lawyer responsible for his losing a suit against a "right of road and the bridge that made a thoroughfare of his land for every vagabond who preferred an opportunity of damaging private property to walking like an honest man along the high road". His unreasoning anger over this matter contributes to his own tragedy and his daughter's.

In *Adam Bede* Hetty Sorrel takes to the footpaths "that she may walk slowly, and not care how her face looks, as she dwells on wretched thoughts", but it is also because she is becoming an outlaw, about to give birth to an illegitimate child and then kill it. It is the voice of suspicious respectability that demands of her:

"Why dooant you keep where there's finger-poasses an' folks to ax the way on?"

Hetty has contemplated suicide on the long path leading to the pool in the wood. She reached a low point in her journey of despair, but turned back to the highroad.

Gypsies are a special class of vagrant, and they are particularly associated with green lanes. These were wide enough and sometimes had a sufficiently good surface for a horse and cart, and their wide verges make good camping sites. John Drinkwater wrote a children's poem called *The Gypsy* which begins:

> I saw a Gypsy in the lane
> *It's quite understood*
> *That I never should*
> *Play with the gypsies in the wood* –
> Nevertheless,
> I must confess,
> That *I did see a Gypsy in the lane*.

Today the gypsy style of life has altered like most other people's to become more urban. Their car-drawn caravans need metalled roads. Many of what were once green lanes are now metalled in any case, but we walk the ones that remain without coming on the sight that Gay saw, and Borrow, and Miss Mitford, and Maggie Tulliver, and Little Nell, and Richard Jefferies, and Edward Thomas. Llewelyn Powys in *Somerset and Dorset Essays* recalls the old gypsy woman Nancy Cooper who figures also in several of his brother John's novels. He quotes a poem John wrote inspired by her which speaks of:

> The road that from Hawk's Hill to Green Lane Hollows
> Is nought but rabbits and cuckoos and swallows
> And fields with turnip sowed;

and goes on:

> Dearie I! the road that over
> Badger's Warren and Turnstile Hill

Skirts park-fence by Witham's Cover . . .
And leads to Dead Man's Mill . . .

The names show that Powys is here using the word "road"
as Hardy does to mean way or route, and delighting in that
intimate knowledge of place which is strongest in those who
live most out of doors.

Smugglers and poachers used the old roads and footpaths
too. The smugglers would be able to escape detection and
avoid toll-gates. Hardy's poem *Winter Night in Woodland*
harks back to a time when "the poachers, with swingels,
and matches of brimstone," would be after pheasants in one
part of the wood while

Where a path wavers through,
Dark figures, filed singly, thrid quickly the view,
Yet heavily laden: land-carriers are they
In the hire of the smugglers from some nearest bay.

In T. H. White's *Farewell Victoria*, Mundy remembers how:

The Countess had told him about the smugglers' routes as
far inland as Burwash, where the London jobbers came to
buy their goods. Those inland paths ran parallel to the
King's highway, a field or two away from it. They would
cross the horizontal roads perhaps only twice between
Hastings and the Weald. But they were recognised trails,
for which the farmers would leave their gates open . . . It
gave him an obscure joy to think of the human tracks,
secret and woodland and recognised, like the tracks of
rabbits. Humanity! He was full of love.

This kind of use often over the years created a right of way
for the public. Poachers used footpaths to loiter about close
to their game, since they could not be challenged while they
were not actually trespassing. Richard Jefferies has a good
deal to say on the subject, looked at usually from the game-
keeper's point of view, but not without a sneaking admira-
ation on occasion for such characters as Luke, the "rabbit-
contractor". Flora Thompson recalls seeing a lucky bag:

It was near sunset and the low, level light searched the path and the stubble and aftermath on either side of it. The men sauntered along in twos and threes, smoking and talking, then disappeared, group by group, over the stile at the farther side of the field. Just as the last group was nearing the stile . . . a hare broke from one of the hedges and went bounding and capering across the field . . . It looked for a moment as if it would land under the feet of the last group of men . . . but, suddenly, it scented danger and drew up and squatted motionless behind a tuft of green clover a few feet from the pathway. Just then one of the men fell behind to tie his bootlace: the others passed over the stile. The moment they were out of sight, in one movement, the man left behind rose and flung himself over the clover clump where the hare was hiding. There was a short scuffle, a slight raising of dust; then a limp form was pressed into a dinner-basket, and, after a good look round to make sure his action had not been observed, the man followed his workmates.

For the families of the lowest-paid workers in Victorian times the odd rabbit or bird was an essential supplement to the regular diet of potatoes, cabbage and lard, and most men poached occasionally.

Hardy's novel *The Mayor of Casterbridge* has a town setting, and therefore few paths. But when Henchard visits Mr. Fall the conjurer he can get there only by persevering over a difficult route:

The turnpike-road became a lane, the lane a cart-track, the cart-track a bridle-path, the bridle-path a footway, the footway overgrown.

The conjurer's dwelling, like his profession, puts him out on a limb.

All the characters I have mentioned so far have been more or less disreputable. One of Autolycus' disguises was that of a pedlar, and there are many references to rather more reputable pedlars using the paths, and tinkers and others whose jobs took them travelling from village to village or from farm to farm. Wordsworth's tinker went "through meadows, over stiles" and Mary Webb's Crockman chooses quiet lanes and hill-tracks. One of Alison Uttley's tales for children, which if they are occasionally sentimental, none-theless are furnished with a background of real country knowledge, describes an old track:

> Once this had been an ancient road through the woods, but times had changed and people went along the new road in the valley, leaving the footpath to itself . . . Some-times the pedlar went through the wood on his way from one village to another, for he found the way cooler and softer for his feet.

Lastly, I should mention two unusual wanderers, because both were associated by name with the vagrants. One is W. H. Davies, the "super-tramp", so much of whose poetry speaks of the green and quiet world of the old paths:

> Seek me no more where men are thick,
> But in green lanes where I can walk
> A mile, and still no human folk
> Tread on my shadow . . .

He loved to walk with no companion but his Fancy: with her he would:

> . . . walk green lanes, so still and lone
> That Reynard walked them without hurry, and
> Felt safer than in woods; down some green lane
> That's only ten feet wide, and only one
> Foot in the centre white; which is the time
> When June, with her abundant leaves and grass
> Makes narrow paths of lanes.

The other is Matthew Arnold's Scholar Gypsy who haunted footpaths too, shunning company, glimpsed as he would:

> . . . cross a stile into the public way. . . .
> And once, in winter, on the causeway chill
> When home through flooded fields foot-travellers go
> Have I not passed thee on the wooden bridge. . . .?

asks the poet. The Gypsy's enigmatic figure, part ghost and part tramp, mysterious and outside society, is a fitting one with which to end the chapter.

6

"Solvitur Ambulando"

*S*OLVITUR *ambulando* – the old Latin tag means something like "You can sort it out by walking". Working
out, finding out, unknotting and freeing are all possible connotations of the word *solvitur*, and in this chapter I want to
look at the claims of certain writers for the benefits of
footpath walking to the spirit. Andrew Young used the
words in his poem *A Traveller in Time*:

> Where was I? What was I about to see?
> *Solvitur ambulando.*
> A path offered its company.

A companionable path was more apt for a curative release
than a road, since solitude, peace, and close contact with
nature, as well as the action of walking, are all important
ingredients. Problems unravel as the feet cover the miles,
but through the body's surroundings, as well as the body's
action. The nineteenth-century walking essayists like Hazlitt
frequently used country roads, and of course before tarmac
the distinction between road and path was often simply
between the greater and the less. G. M. Trevelyan began his
famous essay on walking with the words: "I have two
doctors, my left leg and my right" – but even this no-
nonsense rambler reckoned mental as well as physical
benefits were derived from walking. We know from Helen

Thomas's autobiography that Edward used to plunge off cross-country to wrestle with his black devil of depression. It was not always successful, but it was his instinctive attempt at a cure. He himself tells us nothing of the psychic struggles he underwent at such times, but his few crystalline poems testify to some of his hard-won triumphs.

Wilfrid Scawen Blunt records in *A Day in Sussex* how he took lasting nourishment from the countryside:

> I left the dusty high road, and my way
> Was through deep meadows, shut with copses fair.
> A choir of thrushes . . .
> Mild, moon-faced kine . . .
> And hares unwitting close to me did pass.
> Oh, what a blessed thing that evening was! . . . .
> It glimmers yet across whole years like these.

Meredith, in his *Stave of Roving Tim*, sees walking as a good opportunity for thinking, just as Hazlitt did. Elsewhere he associates country walking with man's unfallen state: in *Song* he says:

> My Soul is singing with the happy birds,
> And all my human powers
> Are blooming with the flowers,
> My foot is on the fields and downs . . .

and in *Woodland Peace* he claims:

> No paradise is lost for them
> Who foot by branching root and stem.

He obviously liked to walk alone, which may explain why he never became a member of Stephen's Tramps. A route back to paradisal innocence is an element in what many of these writers were looking for along the paths. Perhaps this crowning gift of the country ways can be summed up in Edmund Blunden's words from his book *English Villages*:

> . . . peace, or sweet content . . . the scene to which the by-way or bridlepath leads us is peculiarly communicative of such a blessing.

The Valley Thick with Corn and detail: Samuel Palmer.

Several passages in Cowper's poem *The Task* sing the praises of country walking, and he rejoices that he has the physical health to make it possible:

> For I have loved the rural walk through lanes
> Of grassy swarth, close cropt by nibbling sheep,
> And skirted thick with intertexture firm
> Of thorny boughs . . .

He was one whose walks sometimes helped to keep his moods of depression at bay. He would have enjoyed, could he have known it, the poetry of a fellow-sufferer from melancholia, John Clare.

Whereas William Barnes loved the paths chiefly in their social aspects, for leading him to other people, Clare, who valued them equally, did so for their retiredness. Although there is a good deal in his poetry about the use of country paths and lanes by schoolboys, farm people going to work or taking Sunday strolls, folk going to fairs, and courting couples, his own chief use for them seems to have been to enjoy "all the deliciousness of solitude". The *Autobiography* tells how he got a bad name for seeking this on Sundays when everyone else was at church. Without probing too deeply into Clare's sad psyche, it is clear that much of his anxiety arose from his family responsibilities and his relationship as "peasant-poet" with the world of letters and patronage. So his solitary walks came to give him not only quiet contact with the nature he loved, but also a temporary escape from pressure. A sequence of sonnets, *Footpaths* I–V, are among the many places where he celebrates the quiet beauties of his intimately known and deeply loved countryside.

But there is nonetheless a pathetic nervous irritation in his writing of the "unwelcome spire" seen while "the mind/ Yearns for a dwelling in so sweet a place" as the wood. This first glimpse of the village along his path signifies the inexorable return to human beings and the unwelcome load of responsibility. The word "mind" too, which recurs so frequently with a troubled note in the *Autobiography* betrays the emotion in what the prim, trim sonnet form almost disguises as conceit. However, in the following sonnet he is persuading himself to enjoy the "calm pleasures" of the sight of the farm with its "russet stacks" and apples for the winter, a sight which in its reassuring homeliness makes "banished fancies full amends".

So were Clare's rambles sovereign for his mind?

> Mild health, I seek thee; whither? Art thou found
> Mid daisies sleeping in the morning dew,
> Along the meadow paths where all around
> May smells so lovely?

Not always. Even when he finds that the paths he remembers "all remain as then they were" (and another cause of sadness was that they often did not), they no longer work the same cure:

> . . . the paths to joy are so worn out
> I can't find one agen.

It is pitiful how the poetry collapses under this mood – "worn out" is a most unapt image, though a revealing one. Wordsworth's same feeling – "the things that I have seen I now can see no more" – produced one of his best, if not the greatest of his poems, his *Ode on the Intimations of Immortality*. Wordsworth was able to transform the sadness of his loss into a new kind of joy. Clare wanted favourable circumstances and strength of mind to do likewise; he never achieved "the philosophic mind". "I had a joy", wrote Clare, "and keep it still alive":

> Of hoarding up in memory's treasured book
> Old favourite spots that with affections thrive.

These spots, like the hatch gate into the wood, or the bending footplanks, become familiar to us in reading his poems. He was not always able to rely on memories of these places as a shelter from psychological storms, as Wordsworth and John Cowper Powys both did. But actual walks, except at the worst times, held much good magic for him:

> I love to walk the fields; they are to me
> A legacy no evil can destroy;
> They, like a spell, set every rapture free
> That cheered me when a boy.

That Wordsworth did manage to hoard the treasured moments of his walks is well known. In *Lines Written Above Tintern Abbey* he claimed that he owed to them:

> In hours of weariness, sensations sweet,
> Felt in the blood, and felt along the heart;
> . . . such, perhaps,
> As have no slight or trivial influence
> On that best portion of a good man's life,
> His little, nameless, unremembered, acts
> Of kindness and of love.

Wordsworth felt the beneficent influence of country walking to extend beyond healing to the positive accumulation of virtue. Alone or with his sister Dorothy or his friend Coleridge he spent a good deal of his life walking about the countryside and writing poetry:

> . . . o'er paths and fields
> In all that neighbourhood, through narrow lanes
> Of eglantine, and through the shady woods,
> And o'er the Border Beacon, and the Waste
> Of naked Pools, and common Crags that lay
> Expos'd on the bare Fell, was scatter'd love,
> A spirit of pleasure and youth's golden gleam.

"Wordsworth's legs," noted De Quincey in *Literary and Lake Reminiscences* "were pointedly condemned by all female connoisseurs," but he goes on:

. . . with these identical legs Wordsworth must have traversed a distance of 175,000 to 180,000 English miles . . . to which . . . he was indebted for a life of unclouded happiness, and we for much of what is most excellent in his writings.

Yet there is little in his poetry about actual paths. One reason is in the nature of the landscape and land use in the Lake District. Much of the hillside was, and remains, open and unenclosed sheep pasture which had fairly general access even if it was not common. In this kind of countryside there are paths, convenient routes which the majority of people use:

> . . . shaped by a simple wearing of the foot
> On rural business passing to and fro . . .
>
> *Excursion VIII*

But there may be several alternatives, and paths of this kind are unlikely to command the same strength of attachment through association as a clearly defined path which provides a unique means of access. The other reason is in Wordsworth. He drew his inspiration from nature, but never from humanised nature. His imagination responded to the large features of the natural landscape and the effects of the elements, to crags and clouds and cataracts. The violet by the mossy stone and the running hare pleased him too. But paths with their stiles and bridges, together with flocks, herds, arable fields, houses and gardens, show man contending with nature and organising it; and for Wordsworth nature, though genial, was too powerful to be tamed.

The more homely Dorothy, Wordsworth's sister, recorded in her Journals their daily walks at Alfoxden in Somerset, and afterwards at Grasmere, along with details of the household tasks of cooking, laundering and sewing, washing her hair and gardening. It is a matter for note if, because of ill health or bad weather, they fail to take a walk. Sometimes a visit or some small errand would be part of the object, but more often the walk itself, for its own sake, was the object. One has the impression that the scenery and exercise afforded them an essential spiritual recharging, performed as naturally as eating. Wordsworth used foot-

A Winter Morning (detail): Joseph Farquharson.

paths almost daily, but he was not a poet of rural ways. His people are often solitaries, or in some way outside the circle of ordinary social intercourse. They have often been defeated by nature, rather than mastering it. That line of his that everyone knows:

> I wandered lonely as a cloud

give us clues to the poet's relationship with the countryside. "Wandered" suggests that he did not stick to a path; "lonely" conveys his isolation and detachment from other people; and a "cloud" does not touch the ground. It is only those poets whose feet are firmly on the ground and who feel themselves to be in touch with the earth and with their fellow-men who acknowledge their debt to the paths.

In prose, it is different. Wordsworth's *Guide to the Lakes* constantly recommends the traveller to take to his legs, and gain the benefits of the routes that will then be open to him. "The Waterfalls of Rydal", he writes:

. . . are pointed out to everyone. But it ought to be observed here, that Rydal-mere is nowhere seen to advantage from the *main road* . . . A foot road passing behind Rydal Mount and under Nab Scar to Grasmere, is very favourable to views of the Lake and the Vale, looking back towards Ambleside. The horse road also, along the Western side of the Lake, under Loughrigg Fell, . . . does justice to the beauties of this small mere, of which the traveller who keeps the high road is not at all aware.

Although much of Wordsworth's poetry describes the exaltation of the soul in the midst of natural landscape, paths, the homely means to this exaltation, are mentioned in passing, but indifferently. But the following passage from his *Guide* leaves us in no doubt not only that he was intimate with the footpaths, but that he understood their origins and history, that he appreciated their value as guides to the best in the countryside, and that his poetry must owe much to them:

Till within the last sixty years there was no communication between any of these vales by carriage-roads: all bulky articles were transported on pack-horses. Owing, however, to the population not being concentrated in villages, but scattered, the valleys themselves were intersected as now by innumerable lanes and pathways leading from house to house and from field to field. These lanes, where they are fenced by stone walls, are mostly bordered with ashes, hazels, wild roses, and beds of tall fern, at their base; while the walls themselves, if old, are overspread with mosses, small ferns, wild strawberries, the geranium, and lichens . . . It is a great advantage to the traveller or resident, that these numerous lanes and paths, if he be a zealous admirer of Nature, will lead him on into all the recesses of the country, so that the hidden treasures of its landscape may, by an ever-ready guide, be laid open to his eyes.

"Sunken treasures" is the phrase John Cowper Powys uses to describe his memories, of inestimable value to him, of vivid moments in the fields. Llewelyn Powys too uses the term in an essay called *The Memory of One Day* which describes a walk near Ringstead through "a legendary sea valley with its stiles built of old oars". One of the more beneficent influences which their father, the formidable Vicar of Montacute, brought to bear on the Powys children was to impart to them a great love for the little things in nature and a habit of taking long walks. Appropriately, Llewelyn describes his father's character in terms of a foot-path image. "Until the hour of his death", he wrote, "the Tao, or way of life that my father followed remained as clear to him as the field-path from Montacute to Lufton, a field-path chequered perhaps with shadows, but leading on and on, pleasantly enough, from stile to sheep-washing pool as plain as day". The "Tao" of his eldest son John was by no means so clear to him, although it became increasingly so as he grew older; but it included from his infancy the harvesting of a particular kind of spiritual food to store and feed on in leaner times. For this he owed a debt to his father, who took him on cross-country walks from an early age, showing him butterflies, rocks and plants. English country walking played a considerable part in John's life and writings: the fact that much of his life was lived and his writing done in America testifies to his notable hoarding ability. "Deep has that West Dorset countryside sunk into my soul!" he wrote in the *Autobiography*.

One of his recollections of early infancy in the Peak District was a footpath across fields near a pine-tree. On moving to Dorset he became, like many imaginative children, absorbed in the pursuit of a "Beatific Vision", which pursuit he called his "Quest". He speaks of the "many paths" along which it led him. One was "a field-path leading out of the Weymouth Road . . . where there was a big fallen willow-tree". On their first day at prep. school his father took him and his brother Littleton across Sherborne Park by a field-path they soon came to know well. He and Littleton spent all their free time in wandering about the countryside in the direction of home. He remembers in particular that "above the Honeycomb Woods there were . . . some extremely pleasant meadow-lands with a right-of-way footpath leading through them . . . In a thick-set hedge near this path grew . . . a magnificent oak-tree". He walked at Cambridge, and records from that time the kind of entranced physical and mental state which contributes to the resolution of problems and tensions:

> . . . the field-dung upon my boots, the ditch-mud plastered thick, with little bits of dead grass in it, against the turned up ends of my trousers, the feel of my oak-stick "Sacred" . . . the salty taste of half-dried sweat upon my lips, the delicious swollenness of my fingers, the sullen sweet weariness of my legs, the indescribable happiness of my calm, dazed, lulled, wind-drugged, air-drunk spirit, were all, after their kind, a sort of thinking, though of *exactly what*, it would be very hard to explain.

In Sussex where he first worked, he records feeling ecstatically happy following a path across some fields beyond Old Shoreham, and at Waringore, he tells us, he remembers "thinking perfectly well to myself as I trod this path, that . . . just to be able to stare at this green moss, at these fallen twigs, at these blood-stained funguses, was sufficient reward for having been born upon this cruelty-blasted planet!"

It is experiences like these which provide for his Wessex novels background description and psychological inter-action with nature, and many of his characters are partly autobiographical. The climax of *Wolf Solent* comes when the hero, saddened by failing to live up to his own principles and by his wife's infidelity, finds that his power of summoning a mental picture of some quintessentially rural scene has left him. This power has always before supported him through bad times. Blindly and automatically he sets out walking; for the time being life has lost all meaning:

He emerged into a narrow, unused cart-track between overgrown, neglected hedges. As he made his way down this path, treading upon young nettles and upon old burdocks, he couldn't help thinking how charged with a secret life of its own, different from all other places, a deserted lane like this was! 'What a world in itself!' he muttered, 'any little overgrown path! The curious satis-faction which this secluded cart-track gave him caused him to stand still in the middle of the path. The hedges sheltered him from the wind. The spirit of the earth called out to him from the green shoots beneath his feet. Faint bird-notes kept sounding from unseen places . . .

Gradually, as he walks, he gets back his sense of proportion, and is nerved to face life once more. He indulges in a fantasy in which he meets Jesus by the stile on Babylon Hill and reassures Him that men do have the power to forget the evil in the world.

In *A Glastonbury Romance* Powys associates footpaths with the values he wishes to endorse, and people he wishes us to like. Nelly and the children use them in preference to roads, which are associated with Philip Crow and the ugly, destructive forces of "progress". The saintly Sam Dekker and his father use them to cross the marshes and visit Nell Zoyland; Philip Crow always drives a car or even flies an aeroplane. Cordelia Geard takes her obsessed and unhappy husband for footpath walks as a part of her attempt to heal him. Powys equates a liking for paths with simplicity, innocence and goodness.

At the end of that rapturous and inspiriting work his *Auto-biography*, he expresses his philosophical insights at the age of sixty, as he was about to return to this country after thirty years in America. His life as an itinerant lecturer had been as nearly rootless as possible, which may explain the dedicated canonisation of certain childhood memories. Nevertheless, in spite, or perhaps because, of his essential solitariness even when surrounded by friends, he had come to value a feeling of sinking his loneliness in "the innumerable personalities of all the men and women who for generations had gone up and down" certain lanes and paths or some "clover-scented cattle-track". This communion in solitude seems to be an essential ingredient of "sorting it out by walking", whether the walker feels at one with his predecessors in that place or with the wild life with which he shares it, or simply with the path itself, marked out by human feet.

7

"Sounds and Scents and Seeings"

When the young year is sweetest, when the year
Is a symphony of sounds and scents and seeings . . .
. . . Collins' meadow is the place to walk

wrote Edmund Blunden. At all times of the year, and on all
kinds of footpath, the rural writers have recorded the
impressions their rapt senses received. Sometimes we
merely have careful description; but, because of their re-
movedness from the human world and their closeness to
nature, footpaths often induce that contemplative state
which is the soil for visionary experience. The senses are
preternaturally sharpened, as we move closer to the animal
kingdom; but the human soul expands to match, producing
that state of "excited reverie" experienced by Yeats, and by
all artists, and all thoughtful human beings, in agreeable
solitude.

Let us listen to some of the notes in the symphony of
sounds. What better starting-place than Collins' meadow:

> . . . where the Beetle winds
> His small but sullen Horn,
> As oft he rises 'midst the twilight Path,
> Against the Pilgrim born in heedless Hum.
> *Ode to Evening*

It is perhaps for such careful details, unusual at such a period, that Collins has won the especial affection of some twentieth-century readers. Elsewhere in this poem he makes his famous references to the "hamlets brown". Blunden, a fellow-Sussexman and an admirer, records his pleasure on walking to the same viewpoint with some friends and observing that "There were no two ways about it; the hamlets *were* brown."

Clare refers more than once to the sound of bees:

> . . . sweet poets of the summer fields;
> Me much delighting as I stroll along
> The narrow path . . .

and for Jefferies the sound was an expected experience connected with a particular footpath through a park:

> In summer from out of the leafy chambers of the limes there falls the pleasant sound of bees innumerable, the voice of whose trembling wings lulls the listening ear as the drowsy sunshine weighs the eyelid.

On another path he used regularly to be pleased by "the continual noise of young rooks" from nests in the overhead elms.

Then there is the wind, which orchestrates its own set of sounds, from the "rus'len leaves" of Barnes's favourite grassy seat beneath an ash, through the "hufflen winds" that "sheäke the zedge", to the full crescendo described in his poem *Lewth* (Shelter):

> As leäte I did wind up the slope, up in under
> The trees . . .
> The wind, as along in the lea I did wander
> Did huffle hard by an' sound lower a-yonder . . .
> An' there, as the wind-blast did zweep on, an' ramble
> By hedges, a-swingen a swoop on the bramble . . .
> An' down in the meäd roun' the rick wer a reäven,
> > I'd jaÿ in the blast
> > That above me did roar.

The Skylark: David Cox.

Francis Kilvert was one of the many country parsons to have enjoyed walking and observing nature and landscape. He kept pleasant and copious diaries, full of footpaths. On a quieter night he was out walking, and recorded:

> 16 July. As I walked along the fieldpath I stopped to listen to the rustle and solemn night whisper of the wheat, so different to its voice by day.

The noise of water is not uniquely available on footpaths, any more than the noise of the wind. Nevertheless the footpaths have afforded opportunities to hear, and enjoy amid the quietness, certain sounds which writers have found worthy of note. Here is Jefferies, who loved his countryside in all weathers, listening to a February thaw:

Released from the grip of the frost, the streams trickle forth from the fields and pour into the ditches, so that while walking along the footpath there is a murmur all round coming from the rush of water.

A certain plank bridge across a brook was one of Clare's special places: he loved everything about it including the sound of the water. In *Recollections of an Evening Walk* he remembers how he:

> . . . listen'd well-pleas'd to the guggles and groans
> The water made passing the pebbles and stones.

As well as the sounds produced by nature Clare grew attached to the familiar sound of certain gates on his favourite paths, and frequently refers to them in his poems, the "creaking gate" and the gate into the wood which clapped shut behind you:

> The riding gate, sharp jerking round,
> Follow'd fast my heels again,
> While echo mockt the clapping sound,
> And 'clap, clap' sang the woods amain.

Above all, the listening walker is likely to be conscious of the sounds produced by his own movements. Greensward produces a delightful absence of sound, at any rate to human ears, but there are many other kinds of surface, and corn to be brushed, or brambles scraped through. Barnes wrote a poem called *Soft Sounds* noticing many little country-side noises, including the sound of feet "sis sis . . . o'er frosty ground . . . on leaves and bentgrass wither'd white", and again "sis sis . . . our footsteps on the hay/Did sound along our summer way". Cobbett, who was always on the move and alive to the nature of roads even though The Thing gave him no leisure to read Gilbert White, noticed how "even in a *green lane*" the horses' hooves on the flint bridle path "made a sound *like hammering*". "Underfoot by the stiles the fallen acorns crunch," wrote Richard Jefferies, and Leigh Hunt remembered:

Making the kicked clover and buttercups
Hiss with the edges of our shoes.

The Lonely Plough by Constance Holme is not a good book, but it has some genuine country knowledge and observation in it, and it is interesting as an example of the literature of rural nostalgia which Raymond Williams found in each generation, each feeling that theirs is the last to see and value a vanishing way of life. The author describes a certain green lane which epitomises her picture of the changing countryside. Along it the countryman loves to walk and be quiet:

> You did not use this lane as a muscular training-ground or a mere short cut; you crept along it on tiptoe and caught it unawares . . . As you walked you heard all sorts of bewitching sounds above and around you, sounds you had known always and sounds you never heard anywhere else. You knew, for instance, the slur of the plough, the whistle of the blackbird, the whirr of the grass-cutter, the slash of the bill-hook on a far fence, the gnawing of turnips, the wind-talk of dead leaves. But there were others you never placed . . .

This peace is shattered by the approach of a girl newly-arrived from town in her motor-car, and we await the unfolding of the standard theme of her countrification. One cannot but reflect sadly that even if *she* learnt that such lanes are better walked than driven along, still thousands of such lanes were tarred and their little, magical noises lost.

> The sweetness of the air coming from the Downs, after the close yet chilly atmosphere of the church, was in itself an exquisite pleasure

to Richard Jefferies. His downland air had a hint of thyme about it, a smell which Miss Mitford also enjoyed on one of her walks along "a mere narrow cart-track, sinking between high banks clothed with fern, and furze, and low broom, crowned with luxuriant hedgerows, and famous for their summer smell of thyme". One of Clare's favourite paths led through a bean-field. He writes about it in several poems, and in *The Field Path* he seems to follow the path further, through the beans, and then into another field, following the hedge, in which cut hay is drying:

> The beans in blossom with their spots of jet
> Smelt sweet as gardens wheresoever met;
> The level meadow grass was in the swath;
> The hedge-brier rose hung right across the path,
> White over with its flowers; the grass that lay
> Bleaching beneath the twittering heat to hay
> Smelt so deliciously, the puzzled bee
> Went wondering where the honey sweets could be;
> And passer-by along the level rows
> Stoopt down and whipt a bit beneath his nose.

We must not suppose that the monochrome path can offer no delight to the eye. Among the generally muted or sombre colours of the English countryside the sudden· splash or dash of bright pigment in kingfisher or poppy will take the sense by storm and ravish where heaped variety of colour would scarcely stir it. In living tissue the colour is infinitely subtle. We have all experienced a sense of wonder in gazing at the human iris we term blue, or brown, or green, and observing it to be made up of many colours. So it is with feather, fur, and flower and leaf. Wizardry has often been clothed in a garment of shifting colours; such is the natural magic of every living thing. Here is Richard Jefferies on a path through a corn-field (the kind farmers are always particularly anxious to close):

> Pure colour almost always gives the idea of fire, or, rather, it is perhaps as if a light shone through as well as the colour itself. The fresh green blade of corn is like this – so pellucid, so clear and pure in its green as to seem to shine with colour.

Clare's yellow pile-wort had made him think of fire too: he sees it growing in the green lane where it "blazes out/

A Scene in the Isle of Wight: Richard Burchett.

Enough to burn the fingers". And here is Jefferies walking beside the wheat later in the year:

> The path ran for a mile beside it – a mile of wheat in one piece – all those million million stalks the same height, all with about the same number of grains in each ear, all ripening together. The hue of the surface travelled along as you approached; the tint of yellow shifted farther like a reflection of sunlight on water, but the surface was really much the same colour everywhere.

Again the experience has been elemental – water this time, instead of fire.

Jefferies' description of the footpath through the orchards is an example of his landscape painting in words:

> Though the path really is in shadow as the branches shut out the sun, yet it seems brighter here than in the open, as if the place were illuminated by a million tiny lamps shedding the softest lustre. The light is reflected and apparently increased by the countless flowers overhead.

Clare's poem *The Wheat Ripening* gives the colours with painterly accuracy:

> What time the wheat-field tinges rusty brown
> And barley bleaches in its mellow grey,
> 'Tis sweet some smooth-mown baulk to wander down
> Or cross the fields on footpath's narrow way.

The placid Miss Mitford is never startled out of herself by beauty: she never sees visions or dreams dreams. Her description of autumn colours is *pleasant* and *pretty*, just as she intended, without being ecstatic:

> A slight frost had strewed the green lane with the light yellow leaves of the elm – those leaves on whose yielding crispness it is so pleasant to tread . . . whilst the reddened beech and spotted sycamore, and the rich oaks dropping with acorns, their foliage just edging into its deep orange-brown, added all the magic of colour to the original beauty of the scenery. It was undoubtedly the prettiest walk in the neighbourhood, and the one which I frequented the most.

Sometimes it is a touch of colour, especially the first spring flower, that takes the sense, as it does Dud Noman's in Powys's *Maiden Castle*:

> Glancing at the ditch . . . he suddenly stopped with a sharp spasm of delight. *There was the first celandine!*

Our pale suns and clouded skies make colours muted, so that the occasional bright one strikes the eye as exotic; this is reflected in Leigh Hunt's "alley green, with poppies edged . . . where sails the long blue fly". Sometimes the colour of the path itself has struck the writer, as it did in Barnes's poem *Green*. In *The Return of the Native* Hardy describes the purple and brown heath across which "the white flints of a footpath lay like a thread". In *Sons and Lovers* Lawrence describes a "wet, red track". Here is how E. M. Forster paints the bridleway in *The Longest Journey* on which Rickie and Stephen go riding together:

Beneath these colours lurked the unconquerable chalk,
and wherever the soil was poor it emerged. The grassy
track, so gay with scabious and bedstraw, was snow-
white at the bottom of its ruts.

This is the same Wiltshire chalk that Richard Jefferies so
often wrote about.

From a tiny visual detail, such as Barnes's noticing the
"gil'cup-meal" on people's shoes, or Jefferies' observation
that the way a stalk appears through the leaf of a pea is like a
thumb thrust through a palette, all the way to a panoramic
description of a view, the footpath has given writers vision.
"From this elm-pole stile, overshadowed by curving hazel
wands", wrote Edward Thomas:

> . . . the eye travels over a wide landscape of sloping
> meadow, furze, and woodland. Grey pastures undulate
> to the horizon, hedged in by hawthorns, with here and
> there a dark yew or wind-shaken oak. In the green
> coombe beneath us tall elms, purpling with buds, tower
> above the meadow. Past them, and through a briar hedge,
> winds the path – a thin line faintly drawn across fields of
> vale and windy upland.

This kind of wide prospect is one which rural landscape
paintings often provide, the footpath sometimes affording
both a viewpoint and a part of the subject-matter. Here
Thomas gives us a picture in words. A heightened passage
in Francis Kilvert's diary captures the sights, and also the
sounds, of evening from another path which commanded a
view:

> From the stile on the top of the hill above the plantation
> watched the sun set in a crimson ball behind the hills or
> rather into a dense ball of dark blue vapour. It was like
> seeing a sunset over the sea. He went down very fast. All
> the country round was full of evening sounds, children's
> voices, dogs barking, the clangour of geese. Meanwhile
> the sheep fed quietly round me. Then came the afterglow
> round the South and East. Scarlet feathers floated in the

sky, and the gorse deepened into a richer redder gold in the sunset light.

It would be possible to compile a complete anthology of pure description of footpaths, and a good one too. In this chapter especially I have had to select; but the reader will find other examples for himself. Once alerted to the connection between footpaths and "seeings" he will be astonished at the variety and multitude of, in the words of Kirke White, "what rural objects steal upon the sight". Flora Thompson ended her country life and her childhood by a period as a postwoman. She had one of the most rural rounds, and her description of how she took away the memory of this mental landscape to feed upon in after years gives expression to what many have felt but been dumb to say:

> On the last morning of her postwoman's round, when she came to the path between trees where she had seen the birds' footprints on the snow, she turned and looked back upon the familiar landmarks. It was a morning of ground mist, yellow sunshine, and high rifts of blue, white-cloud-dappled sky. The leaves were still thick on the trees, but dew-spangled gossamer threads hung on the bushes and the shrill little cries of unrest of the swallows skimming the green open spaces of the park told of autumn and change . . . The pond where the yellow brandyball water-lilies grew, the little birch thicket where the long-tailed tits had congregated, the boathouse where she had sheltered from the thunderstorm and seen the rain splash like leaden bullets into the leaden water, and the hillock beyond from which she had seen the perfect rainbow. She was never to see any of these again, but she was to carry a mental picture of them, to be recalled at will, through the changing scenes of a lifetime.

Such mental landscapes have been among people's most treasured possessions, and Wordsworth is not the only poet whose inspiration sprang from beloved scenes experienced with heightened emotion and "recollected in tranquility"

Landscape paintings, or other pictures with a country setting, give pleasure by their subject-matter to many who know nothing of the principles of art but who enjoy the reminiscence of having seen such things in nature. Richard Jefferies, that great landscape painter in words, writes scathingly of those who pander to a sentimental taste for the rural uneducated by the real thing. He unburdens himself in *Amaryllis at the Fair* by way of illustrating the truthfulness of his character Alere, the artist:

> In a whole saloon of water colours, in a whole Academy, or Grosvenor Gallery, you shall find hardly three works that represent any real scene in the fields. I have walked about the fields a good deal in my brief, fretful hour, yet I have never seen anything resembling the strange apparitions that are hung on these walls every spring. Apparitions – optical illusions, lit up with watery, greenish, ghastly, ghost-light – nothing like them on earth I swear . . . Touched up designs; a tree taken from one place, a brook from another, a house from another – *and mixed to order*, like a prescription by the chemist – xv.grs. grass, 3 dr. stile, iiij. grs. rustic bridge.

We might not all have the power to distinguish pure spring water from the chemist's draught: that "3 dr. stile, iiij. grs.rustic bridge" suggests there are paths in both. The word "prescription" is revealing, suggesting a need for such things to keep us in health, just as we need to take physic if our physical diet is impoverished.

A visit to the Tate Gallery's Constable exhibition in 1976 brought home to me how many of his paintings are of or from rights of way. Think of the *The Corn Field*. The field is shown through a gap in the hedge and an open gate off a lane, the one down which a flock of sheep is disappearing. Attfield Brooks in *Constable and his Country* gives us the benefit of his explorations to find the painter's exact viewpoints – there was no chemist's draught mixed in Constable's case – and of *Autumnal Sunset* he writes:

Autumnal Sunset: John Constable.

The scene is from the lane leading down from East Bergholt Post Office to Vale Farm. Just inside the farm gate the lane becomes private but the footpath continues to Stratford St. Mary Church. The path has been diverted in recent years so that instead of proceeding across the middle of the fields as shown in the painting it continues along the lane towards the farm and up the side of the further field. In . . . 1963, the remains of the stile in the valley and the track of the old path across the ploughed field . . . (were) just visible.

Many pre-Raphaelite pictures feature actual fieldpaths, even though the treatment may be characteristically coloured and symbolic. Paul Nash in his autobiography *Outline* describes the fieldpath by which he used to walk to school at Yately in Hampshire, a motif which appears in his paintings:

> On the other side of the stile the path continued under very different conditions. Whereas in the open fields it seemed to run unhindered at top speed, abreast of the hedgerow, it now appeared to falter and creep along in the twilight of the wood. Its colour changed from a bright resilient tone to a purplish brown. Its surface now became heavy, damp and unsure, its form confused by dead leaves and encroaching undergrowth. Here I trod more circumspectly, glancing from side to side. It was very quiet and still.

Painters like Paul Nash and Graham Sutherland, who were friends and contemporaries of the Georgian poets, shared their preoccupation with the cultivated English countryside. But perhaps the pre-eminent footpath artist was the engraver Myles Birket Foster, whose many stiles and lanes are of a piece with his feeling for a friendly, humanised landscape.

Two senses are missing from Blunden's euphonious list, and they should not be forgotten. Clare's:

> . . . rambling bramble-berries, pulp and sweet,

>   Arching their prickly trails
>   Half o'er the narrow lane

shall represent the taste, and his terse simile of the pathway "as wet as a mop" the sense of touch. Before rubber boots were invented anyone who used the paths in all weathers would be acutely conscious of the conditions underfoot. An elderly neighbour of mine told me, "We used to have wet feet most of the time, even in summer. You'd go out early to see after the cattle and the dew'd go right through your boots quicker than anything." To Clare the absence of dew under certain conditions in high summer was therefore noteworthy:

>   And through the grain one's walk may go
>   And not a dewdrop moist the shoe,
>   For not a blade or leaflet green
>   Deckt with a single drop is seen;
>   The deepest woodland path is dry.

And in his second footpath sonnet he records that delightful feeling the wayfarer experiences:

>   As wading to (his) waist in crowding grain
>   Wherever as we pass the bending ears
>   Pat at our sides and gain their place again.

Llewelyn Powys described a walk with his brother John in the countryside around Montacute, following his recovery from one of his attacks of consumption:

Lesser blues and gate-keepers flitted about our boots, the soles of which had been polished so smooth by walking over the fields . . . We trod silently . . . Above Windmill we passed through a field of oats, the green stalks of which had already taken to themselves that amethystine tint characteristic of oat-straw when the grain is approaching maturity.

The extreme alertness of all the senses is very like Richard Jefferies' and may be the gift of those suffering from that disease, or of those who have looked death in the face.

Of all the writers whom the paths inspired, Richard Jefferies stands out as the one who gives us the most careful and loving detail. "They only know a country who are acquainted with its footpaths," he wrote. "By the roads, indeed, the outside may be seen; but the footpaths go through the heart of the land." Jefferies' especial gift as a writer lay in his power to communicate pleasure in the tiniest detail of what he saw, and felt, and heard, as he walked through the heart of the land: his best writings are simply logs, in poetical prose, of footpath walks, where he keeps his eye steadily and quietly on his subject.

The peculiar power of his best writing lies in its accuracy and in the clarity of its vision. He was able to make himself into a subtle instrument for recording impressions; it is as though he himself were the earth of the footpath on which he observed one morning that the sharp, light feet of the birds had printed "an inextricable design". Here is a path from *The Pageant of Summer*:

> There is a mark only now where the footpath was; it passed close to the hedge, but its place is traceable only as a groove in the sorrel and seed-tops. Though it has quite filled the path, the grass there cannot send its tops so high; it has left a winding crease.

This is Jefferies at his plainest. What seems to me so significant about these simple statements? What do we gain in reading these words about an obscure path we have never walked? First we share his feeling for the place; a feeling no less intense for being quietly expressed. He knows it well, for he has seen it at other seasons; he knows from previous experience of the path that it passed close to the hedge. He notes carefully the impression he receives, "a mark . . . a groove in the sorrel and seed-tops . . . a winding crease". This care commands our attention, compels us to share his picture of the path "filled" by the weeds and grass of summer. The plenitude of summer is emphasised by the observation that the tops of the grass were *not* so high when growing from the hard-packed or perhaps slightly sunken path. The path seems to maintain a touch of austerity, of independence, amid the universal fecundity. Notice the alliteration of "sorrel" and "seed-tops" and then read the whole passage and hear all the repeated esses make the sound of feet swishing through long grass. Notice too the covert tenderness of the way he writes about the grass: it seems sentient. It fills, it sends its tops, it leaves a crease – these phrases suggest a greater dignity and purpose than mere passive growth even though that growth is frustrated. The word "traceable" suggests his close observation of the landscape, searching for clues in it, copying it faithfully *and slowly* – you cannot trace anything in a hurry. Here are many of his secrets in this word.

Jefferies was probably less of an ornithologist than W. H. Hudson, but his *delight* in birds seems to me deeper. He continually conveys his sense of pleasure in their characteristic ways, and at finding them in his and their shared haunts, whether it is the ugly, squawking young rooks, or whether he hears:

> From the bushes by the stile on the left hand, which I have just passed, . . . the long whistle of a nightingale. His nest is near; he sings night and day. Had I waited on the stile, in a few minutes, becoming used to my presence, he would have made the hawthorn vibrate, so powerful is his voice when heard close at hand. There is not another nightingale along this path for at least a mile, though it crosses meadows and runs by hedges to all appearance equally suitable. But nightingales will not pass their limits . . .

Notice his staunchness for truth. He might have fudged the facts and had the bird sing for him: as it is we can share more fully in a slightly incomplete experience.

Andrew Young's poem *The Bird* records sharing a habitat with a kindred simplicity and pleasure:

> Last week, last night; tonight's the third
> Time I have startled the same bird
> Here by field path she has
> Her nest, close in long grass.

On another path Jefferies expects and enjoys the lapwings which "stand on the parallel ridges of the ploughed field like a drilled company". He enjoys too the fact that the paths are used as thoroughfares by creatures other than man:

> There is a plantation of fir and ash on the slope, and a narrow wagon-way enters it, and seems to lose itself in the wood. Always approach this spot quietly, for whatever is in the wood is sure at some time or other to come to the open space of the track. Wood-pigeons, pheasants, squirrels, magpies, hares, everything feathered or furred, down to the mole, is sure to seek the open way. Butterflies flutter through the copse by it in summer, just as you or I might use the passage through the trees. Towards the evening the partridges may run through to join their friends before roost-time on the ground. Or you may see a covey there now and then, creeping slowly with humped backs, and at a distance not unlike hedgehogs in their motions.

Sooner or later reading Jefferies one cannot help but share his excitement at the presence of wild things. Eventually a bare record like this in *Magpie Fields*:

> The last day of August there was a fierce combat on the footpath between a wasp and a brown moth

takes on Homeric status.

Clare too had loved birds, and a series of poems tells of finding nests on footpaths. There was a nightingale's nest near his favourite gate into the wood – "Hush! let the woodgate softly clap," he begs, "for fear/The noise might drive her from her home of love". In *The Pettichap's Nest* he wrote:

> Well! in my many walks I've rarely found

From Shade to Sunshine: Frederick George Cotman.

A place less likely for a bird to form
Its nest – close by the rutted-galled wagon-road
And on the almost bare foot-trodden ground.

Under the footbridge every year he found a swallow's nest, and once was led to a yellow-hammer's when "just by the wooden bridge a bird flew up".

Even Gilbert White, though as vicar of the parish of Selborne and a local naturalist he may have had pretty general access, often mentions in passing in his *Natural History* that he observed a particular species by a path or cart track. Virginia Woolf learned to love footpaths from her father Leslie Stephen, the first secretary of the Commons Society and founder of the Order of Sunday Tramps. In 1917 she was walking almost daily at Asheham in Sussex, and on August 5 she entered in her diary:

> . . . very hot and sunny afternoon. Walked on M's walk. Saw 3 perfect peacock butterflies, 1 silver washed frit[illary]; besides innumerable blues feeding on dung. All freshly out & swarming on the hill. Small flowers out in great quantities. Found mushrooms, mostly in the hollow, enough for a dish.

Her novel *Night and Day*, which was published in 1919, drew on her knowledge of paths and made use of them in significant contexts. Ralph Denham goes down to stay with Mary's family in the country and they walk together across the fields from the station:

> . . . along a path now slightly darker than the dim green surrounding it. In front of them the sky now showed itself of a reddish-yellow, like a slice of some semilucent stone behind which a lamp burnt while a fringe of black trees with distinct branches stood against the light.

The visionary description is intended to enhance the value of the countryside, with which Mary is associated, as opposed to the town. Later as he walks another fieldpath, Denham meditates on a new way of life.

Among the poets, Andrew Young had an especially keen eye for the insect life of the paths, midges, bees, caterpillars – nothing is insignificant to him that has life in it. In his poem *August* he noted how:

> The cows stood in a thundercloud of flies,
> As lagging through the field with trailing feet
> I kicked up scores of skipper butterflies
> That hopped a little way, lazy with heat.

Clare too had loved the insects. In his sonnet *Sabbath Walks* he recorded watching the spider spin between blades of grass, and the "lab'ring ants" and the "'clock-a-clay' pruning its red wings." He entered into the lives and doings of these tiny creatures and so forgot himself awhile.

Richard Jefferies enjoyed the paths even in February, when the mud gave him the chance to see those bird's-foot patterns. Edward Thomas was apt at learning from Jefferies' writings how to use and value footpaths. In his poem *November* Thomas wrote:

> November's earth is dirty,
> Those thirty days, from first to last;
> And the prettiest things on ground are the paths
> With morning and evening hobnails dinted,
> With foot and wing-tip overprinted
> Or separately charactered,
> Of little beast and little bird.

It is the little things that the footpath poets most often sing – little things and the value of them. Thus it was that for Jefferies "there never was a footpath yet which did not pass something of interest". Clare's poem *Field Thoughts* expresses it like this:

> Field thoughts to me are happiness and joy,
> When I can lie upon the pleasant grass
> Or track some little path and so employ
> My mind in trifles . . .

He loved to walk a path "Making oft remarking stops,/

Watching tiny nameless things". Some of the intensity of Keats's later poetry derives from distillations of such ramblings. Like Clare he had stood on a footbridge and watched, as he reccommends us:

> Linger awhile upon some bending planks
> That lean against a streamlet's rushy banks,
> And watch intently Nature's gentle doings.

Andrew Young walked the hill-track at Steyning "where small sticks crack" and where "on hanging spider's thread the sun/Glides to and fro like one who walks/A tight-rope". And Ivor Gurney wrote in his *Walking Song*:

> My comrades are the small
> Or dumb or singing birds,
> Squirrels, field-things all.

His words in *The Escape* express what must have been generally held by all these writers:

> I believe in the increasing of life whatever
> Leads to the seeing of small trifles,
> Real, beautiful, is good . . .

Footpaths gave to him, and to all these rural writers, the chance to see and the peace to enjoy such precious minutiae.

8

"Untrodden Ways"

IN HIS essay *Rural Life in England*, Washington Irving wrote:

> The pastoral writers of other countries appear as if they
> had paid nature an occasional visit, and become acquain-
> ted with her general charms; but the British poets have
> lived and revelled with her – they have wooed her in her
> most secret haunts – they have watched her minutest
> caprices.

This quality in our pastoral writing from Chaucer onwards
he attributes to the interest of the English gentry in country
occupations and to a paternalism upon which he looks with
approval; but there may be other reasons. Most of the
writers referred to in this book have been able to woo
nature in her secret haunts thanks to the access to the
countryside afforded by the paths – helped out by the
occasional trespass. This characteristically English intimacy
with Nature we find in writers who might be called rural,
rather than pastoral – a distinction well drawn by W. J.
Keith in his book *The Rural Tradition*. Broadly, they concern
themselves with a real rather than an ideal countryside,
though this of course does not necessarily imply a grim one.
Raymond Williams refers to the "rural-sexual metaphor" in
writers such as D. H. Lawrence and T. F. Powys, and to
"conscious intercourse with the Earth". The image is no-

where more apparent than in footpath description, since the paths are the physical routes to that intercourse; they penetrate the landscape, and he who explores them is often seen in sexual terms as enjoying secret pleasures. Since they may go anywhere, those who own the countryside are necessarily debarred from the licensed pleasure of the access afforded by a particular path and from the unlicensed pleasure of trespass.

John Cowper Powys's earliest novel *Wood and Stone* uses Auber Lake and the path to it, overhung with dark foliage, as sexually symbolic in the manner we can now easily recognise since Freudian studies of writers like Henry James. "The lane itself," he tells us, "was but a deep shadowy path dividing a flowing sea of foliage, which seemed to pour, in a tidal wave of suffocating fertility, over the whole valley." The point is repeatedly laboured in in-flated language such as this. But the mode Powys came to prefer, where metaphor grows out of a scrupulous realism, is already present in the book:

> (Lacrima) scrambled into a field on the border of the road. Following a little path which led across it, and cross-ing two more meadows, she flung herself down under the shadow of some great elms, in a sort of grassy hollow be-neath an overgrown hedge.

Here Goring, her unwanted wooer and the farmer who owns the land crossed by the path, finds her in tears. However little used the path, her secret place will not be secret to the farmer. Similarly, in *Rodmoor*, Brand means to seduce Linda, who is terrified of the sea:

> The girl's pulses beat a wild excited tune. He led her straight along the narrow, reed-bordered path, with a ditch on either side of it which ended in a bridge across the Loon . . .

'Not to the sea', she pleads, "'Yes, to the sea!'" he replies, masterfully. Powys is still a little heavy-handed.

By the time he came to *Wolf Solent* he had mastered what

he wanted to do. T. F. Powys certainly has some sexually symbolic lanes and paths, and in general, like Llewelyn Powys but with a different flavour, tends to think in obsessively sexual terms; but it was John who wove the idea into the thick psychological and descriptive fabric of a novel and gave it real potency. Wolf's exploration of the countryside and his seduction of Gerda advance simultaneously, and he comes at the same moment to knowledge of the body of each:

> Past poplars and willows, past muddy ditches and wooden dams, past deserted cow-sheds and old decrepit barges half-drowned in water, past tall hedges of white-flowering blackthorn, past low thick hedges of scarcely-budded hawthorn, past stupid large-bodied cattle . . .

he made his way through those pleasant pastures to his tryst. When he has possessed her for the first time:

> when . . . they stood together again outside the hut, there came over him a vague feeling, as if he had actually invaded and possessed something of the virginal aloofness of the now darkened fields.

This passage has reverberations throughout the book. Gerda lying asleep on Babylon Hill seems for the first time unattainable as cold nature; an overgrown lane is "charged with a secret life of its own, different from all other places".

Many a path leads to a woman's dwelling-place, and sexual symbolism is often implicit. In Tennyson's poem *The Gardener's Daughter*, the girl's home is reached by a cross-country walk at the end of which:

> . . . a well-worn pathway courted us
> To one green wicket in a privet hedge.

The "untrodden ways" which led to Wordsworth's Lucy suggest the virgin, waiting to be deflowered. Maidenhood is occasionally preserved: the "satyrs rude" of William Browne's *Britannia's Pastorals*:

Durst not attempt, or e'er intrude
With such a mind the flowery balks
Where harmless virgins have their walks.

And in Victoria Sackville-West's emotional poem *The Land*,
the line:

Private the woods, enjoying a secret beauty

conveys not only a landowner's possessiveness, but a
female sexuality that is nonetheless closed to males.

Of course, the walker does not have to be male. In
Richard Jefferies' novel *The Dewy Morn* Felise is first seen,
and fallen in love with, as a trespasser. Then she learns the
proper country ways, and her exploration of the countryside
coincides with and bodies forth the growth of her relationship with her lover:

She trod the paths to their utmost ending, through meads
and wheatfields, round the skirts of copses where
pheasants feeding hurried in at her coming, or wood-
pigeons rose with a clatter from the firs. Climbing the
rugged stiles, treading the bending plank stretched across
the streamlet, stepping from stone to stone in the watery
ways where woods and marshes met, up the steep hill
where the shepherds had cut steps in the turf, she traced
the path to its ending. Through the long lanes, hazel-
boughs on one side, hawthorn on the other; along the
rude waggon-tracks winding in and out of the corn; by
shadowy green arcades of the covers.

Footpaths are our routes to a licensed intimacy with the
landscape, to a carnal knowledge of nature; and no-one
expresses this more sweetly than Edward Thomas who in
Horae Solitariae thus describes a lane:

. . . it entered gently into the secret places of the land. On
either side the fields and woods lay open; surprised but
not alarmed by so tranquil an intrusion, they were beheld
in all their divinity.

Lingering Autumn: John Everett Millais.

To enter the countryside other than by the public paths is to commit a trespass, a theme frequently explored by D. H. Lawrence, who also makes much of the symbolic connection between illicit access and illicit love. The park in *Lady Chatterley's Lover* has no access. Significantly, it has been closed:

> . . . this riding was an old, old thoroughfare coming across country. But now, of course, it was only a riding through the private wood.

And this wood, Clifford Chatterley says:

> "I consider this is really the heart of England . . . I want this wood perfect . . . untouched. I want nobody to trespass in it.

The conservative landowner and the impotent but possessive husband speak here with one voice. Ironically, of course, it is Mellors, whose job it is to prevent trespass against the one who commits trespass against the other – the now classic example of the gamekeeper turned poacher.

The gentry took their exercise in their own grounds, and when going anywhere tended to drive. Hunting still takes them cross-country at speed and oblivious of recognised routes in panting pursuit of a quarry. It is a formidable *droit de seigneur*, a licensed rape of the countryside. But the more aristocratic the novel therefore, the less we find about footpaths. Thus of all Hardy's novels *Two on a Tower*, though set in Wessex, has fewest mentions of paths, because its heroine is a lady of birth. *Lady Chatterley's Lover* comes into this class, and perhaps owes some slight debt to Meredith's novel *The Egoist*. In both books a young woman is entrapped by an egotistical landowner, and, by extension, his park. In *The Egoist*, as I pointed out earlier, Clara retorted upon Laetitia's conventional praise of the beauty of the private walks, and her rebellion at one point took the form of a literal escape by public footpath to the station. The original of her accepted lover, Vernon Whitford, is said to have been Meredith's friend Leslie Stephen, who sometimes used to descend on Meredith at Box Hill with his band of "Tramps".

Not only in *Lady Chatterley's Lover* but throughout his writings the theme of trespass and exclusion engages Lawrence. In *The White Peacock* Cyril returns in later life to Strelley Mill to find near Woodside "barbed-wire along the path, and at the end of every riding it was tarred on the tree-trunks 'Private'". The freedom of childhood has passed, when one wandered at will. There has even been a half-way stage, when shades of the prison-house began to close, represented in the scene where they trespass in the snowdrop wood, arguing among themselves whether they should, and are confronted by the gamekeeper. More significant still is the appearance in the woods of the errant father who, unknown, is treated as a trespasser by his son: he has foregone his rights in that place. Partly, it is a technical matter; the houses of Nethermere are off the road and linked by private paths, and there is doubt as to public access to the woods. But as so often in Lawrence real land-scapes become charged with symbolic meaning. When Paul and his mother in *Sons and Lovers* first make their way to Willey Farm she is anxious lest the path is private and they should be told off the land. But they are directed pleasantly:

> . . . through the wheat and oats, over a little bridge into a wild meadow. Peewits, with their white breasts glisten-ing, wheeled and screamed about them. The lake was still and blue. High overhead a heron floated. Opposite, the wood leaped on a hill, green and still.

It is Paul who finds the way, saying, "'I can feel a bit of a path this road . . . You've got town feet, somehow or other, you have'" and leads them through a little gate giving onto a flowery path through the fenced and dark wood. His mother's faint distress on this occasion foreshadows her later jealousy and irritation; but Paul has achieved symbolic access to the world of beauty and feeling which is the best part of his relationship with Miriam. In *The Trespasser* it is a public path where Cecil walks with Helena and picks honeysuckle for her; but he commits a trespass just the same, for she walked there before with Siegmund, and it was "his" path. And in *The Shades of Spring* a trespasser enters a beautiful private path, confronts the keeper, and poaches his girl.

There is a considerable mythology surrounding the law on the subject of trespass: "you have only to offer the farmer sixpence if he stops you, and he can't do anything" is a fre-quently asserted belief. It is nonsense. It is true however that you cannot get a conviction for trespass unless damage of some kind can be proved. Where the trespass is simply walking the landowner may go to a lot of trouble in getting his case through the courts and end up with a ha'pennorth of damages, so the game is not often thought worth the candle. Americans I have met cherish an even more thorough-going belief, that they may walk anywhere – a belief which sorts oddly with the barbed wire and hostile notices we saw in 1970 even on parts of the Appalachian Trail.

The law in full dress, whether English or American, is outside my scope; but these popular notions of the law, evincing a belief in the common man's right to cross the land and see it, lie behind many of the literary references to trespass. W. H. Hudson, for instance, in a flow of splendid rhetoric, writes:

> The stream invites us to follow: the impulse is so common that it might be set down as an instinct; and certainly there is no more fascinating pastime than to keep company with a river from its source to the sea. Unfortunately this is not easy in a country where running waters have been enclosed, which should be as free as the rain and sunshine to all, and were once free, when England was England still, before landowners annexed them, even as they annexed or stole the commons and shut up the footpaths.

And Hudson did trespass, despite barbed wire which he called "man's devilish improvement on the bramble". Hudson is one of those country-lovers, like T. H. White and Henry Williamson after him, who see man as an animal species which has disgraced itself, and so, characteristically, he describes his defiance in terms of a wild animal:

> . . . on that way I intend to keep until I have no more strength to climb over fences and force my way through hedges, but like a blind and worn-out badger must take to my earth and die.

The badger has a wild animal's natural right to the land. Hudson's is what one might call the American attitude (not that many a staunch English democratic heart has not shared it). The words "free as the rain and sunshine to all" evince the same belief in natural rights as the words "God's earth" in this passage from Thoreau:

> At present, in this vicinity, the best part of the land is not private property; the landscape is not owned, and the

Bullingstone, Kent 1847: John Middleton.

walker enjoys comparative freedom. But possibly the day will come when it will be partitioned off into so-called pleasure-grounds, in which a few will take a narrow and exclusive pleasure only, – when fences shall be multiplied, and mantraps and other engines invented to confine men to the *public road*, and walking over the surface of God's earth shall be construed to mean trespassing on some gentleman's grounds.

Edward Thomas exemplifies what one might call the English attitude, acknowledging the existence of authority and ownership, backed by the law, but resisting it nonetheless. "Please trespass," he urges us in *The South Country*:

> The English game preserve is a citadel of woodland charm, and however precious, it has only one or two defenders, easily eluded . . .

Just such a citadel is invaded in Grant Allen's novel *The British Barbarians* – the author of the famous *Woman Who Did* is here recommending a different sort of trespass. An urbane visitor from the future comes anthropologizing in the suburban England of the 1890s and cannot believe that so pleasant a flowery wood is not open to all. He then takes the threatening notice board to be evidence of one of the many strange "taboos" in force, and an amusing confrontation ensues between cool investigator and heated landowner. A similar contretemps takes place in *Mr Lucton's Freedom* by Francis Brett Young, in which the hero tastes freedom from the tyranny of his money, and the standard and style of living it imposes, in the company of the redoubtable Bert, a holidaying clerk who is a member of the Ramblers' Association.

Mr Lucton's Freedom was published in 1940, when the famous Ramblers' rallies and struggle to get access to the Derbyshire grouse moors were recent history. These vast open spaces were once permanently closed to the public in the interests of shooting a few weeks in the year. But all through the first part of this century city clerks like Bert had been turning to the countryside for escape from their grey everyday lives. Leonard Bast in E. M. Forster's novel *Howards End* was nearly saved by his walk across Wimbledon Common. Had he been born thirty years later (the book was published in 1910) he would at least have been a member of the Ramblers' Association and attended classes in art appreciation. As it was, his trespass with Helen Schlegel can be seen as an attempt to possess the world of culture and privilege closed to him by birth. H. G. Wells's *The History of Mr Polly* was also published in 1910. In it the hero and his two friends and fellow-apprentices walk the country paths and talk, and knock likewise at the firmly-closed doors of culture. The first half of the book is a survey of Mr Polly's life to his mid-thirties as he sits on a stile and contemplates suicide.

After the First World War things were different. Feudalism waned and the voice of the common man could more easily be heard, asking both for culture and for better access to the countryside. In his book *The Untutored Townsman's Invasion of the Country* (1946), C. E. M. Joad documents the story of the Ramblers' successes, and examines the whole movement for access in the light of the fast-growing urban population. The burden of Joad's book is that the invasion will happen, should happen, that we should not try to do anything to stop it, but that we should try to educate the masses who have become separated from their natural roots into an understanding of how to behave in the countryside. The kind of "education" meted out in the days of Mr. Bast and before was aimed at incalcating respect for property through fear of the authority which owned it. Such fear once learned dies hard. Clare describes how it got in the way of his enjoyment of the countryside:

> I dreaded walking where there was no path
> And prest with cautious tread the meadow swath,
> And always turned to look with wary eye,
> And always feared the farmer coming by;
> Yet everything about where I had gone
> Appeared so beautiful, I ventured on;
> And when I gained the road where all are free
> I fancied every stranger frowned at me,
> And every kinder look appeared to say,
> 'You've been on trespass in your walk today.'
> I've often thought, the day appeared so fine,
> How beautiful if such a place were mine;
> But having naught I never feel alone
> And cannot use another's as my own.

"Having naught" is the tell-tale phrase; for just as middle-class thieves are "cases" where working-class ones are crooks, so gentry are never trespassers as peasants are. D. H. Lawrence points this nice distinction in *The White Peacock*:

> "It is trespassing," said Emily.
> "We don't trespass," Leslie replied grandiloquently.

The inevitable game-keeper appears and inevitably (and improbably) turns out to be no respecter of persons.

Trollope's attitude to the whole question is a study. He loved the countryside, and by and large humanity, and it clearly troubled him that vast tracts of the one should be kept for the exclusive pleasure of so few of the other. So his Barsetshire produces benevolent hereditary squires who do not, it seems, have the selfish attitude to property he associated only with the nouveaux riches. In *Barchester Towers* he describes the public lane that passes the gates of Ullathorne House, and comments:

> Men, when they are acquiring property, think much of such things, but they who live where their ancestors have lived for years do not feel the misfortune. It never occurred either to Mr. or Miss Thorne that they were not sufficiently private, because the world at large might, if it so wished, walk or drive by their iron gates. That part of the world which availed itself of the privilege was, however, very small.
>
> Such a year or two since were the Thornes of Ullathorne. Such, we believe, are the inhabitants of many an English country home. May it be long before their number diminishes.

This was probably wishful thinking, even in Trollope's day. And even then Major Grantly, in *The Last Chronicle of Barset*, knew what is due to property:

> "I'm afraid I'm intruding," he said, lifting his hat. "I came up the path yonder, not knowing that it would lead me so close to a gentleman's house."

Here the novelist recorded truly. Many an ardent property respecter (to use no more political label) even today will feel it wrong to use a path, a public one, although few people use it, and many times more may daily pass his own less sacred residence. But the rejoinder is less convincing:

> "There is a right of way through the fields onto the Guestwick road,"

returns this amiable and Utopian squire,

> "and therefore you are not trespassing in any sense; but
> we are not particular about such things down here, and
> you would be very welcome if there were no right of
> way."

All I can say is, no squire ever took this tone with me –
possibly Major Grantly's being so obviously the gentleman
was in his favour.

I will end with a poem by Andrew Young. It is called
simply *Private*. It does not protest against property; it
reduces it to unimportance with an unparallelled quietness
of tone which is almost godlike – not a god who thunders,
but a still, small voice, a tone which can only be commanded
by a man of upright life and few words, as Andrew Young
was. Set against nature and time man's petty tyrannies and
puny revolts are not only foolish but irrelevant; he is but a
wayfarer, his goods are but lent. To borrow Shakespeare's
phrase, if ever there was "trespass sweetly urg'd", it is here:

> Trespassers will be prosecuted –
> How? By whom? Who has the right? –
> Hush, go your way; let lip be muted
> With finger; trees will screen from sight –
>
> Then who has placed this notice-board? –
> No one; myself; what matter who?
> The one who claims to be landlord
> Of this hill coppice and path through,
>
> Each cracking stick loose flint and all
> Wild flowers, untenanted snail shell.
> White butterflies that rise and fall,
> Round holes of rabbits and all else.
>
> But why dispute? Thick crowd the leaves;
> Deeper sleeps the moss across the trunk;
> Wayfarer notes on thorn-stabbed sleeves
> Green caterpillar's arching back.

Ten years from now at most a score
This tangled pathway will be lost,
And where its owner walked before
Moonlight will stumble like a ghost.

9

"I Know that This Was Life"

THE image of life as a journey is so old and so pervasive that it is easy to forget it is one; but there is yet great emotional power in the contrast between a grim journeying and a state of house-keeping, settled content towards which, or out from which, the traveller goes. English rural writers have often visualised the road of life as a country footpath, and it is their mental images of this path that I explore in this chapter. It is the image that comes naturally to them, as it did to the cottage preacher Richard Jefferies describes in *Wild Life in a Southern County*. Jefferies reports how he luridly transported the Inquisition into the English countryside in his preaching, with the bound victim dragged along a footpath, exhorted to recant at the first stile, and tortured at the next.

For a Christian there is only one right path, and it is a hard one. "Enter ye in at the strait gate," runs the gospel:

> . . . for wide is the gate, and broad is the way, that leadeth to destruction, and many there be that go in thereat: Because strait is the gate, and narrow is the way, which leadeth into life, and few there be that find it.

Footpaths, less frequented than highroads, impossible for the wealthy to use in their carriages, and often fraught with physical hazards, clearly fitted the metaphor well. The passage seems to have been misunderstood since its translation into English, for "strait" (even when spelt "straight") is being used as a synonym for narrow, as we still use it in our phrase "straitened circumstances", and does not mean, as Bunyan took it, "straight as a rule can make it". It was in any case the gate, and not the way, that was so described – an image reiterated in the saying of the camel and the needle's eye. Shakespeare's Henry IV says penitently:

> God knows, my son, by what by-paths and indirect
> Crooked ways I met the crown

and the image here is of deviousness, of a kind of underhand, nefarious business that takes place off the main road among the Autolycuses. Presumably the same idea lies behind the Tudor proverb, "A man must not leave the King's Highway for a by-way". Nowadays we use the words "devious" and "straightforward" of people's characters or, more crudely, "crooked" and "straight" of their actions, and all these contain a buried metaphor. Can it be that they all stem from this same misunderstanding of the gospel? Whether or no, the notion of directness has our approval, and it is hard to imagine it otherwise.

But it has a confusing effect on the topography of *The Pilgrim's Progress*, which by many touches conveys a picture of a real English landscape complete with footpaths – the wicket gate just discernible on the far side of what turns out to be a very boggy field, the stile into the meadow which leads to Doubting Castle, the "fine, pleasant green lane" along which Ignorance comes, and the three sturdy rogues coming along Deadman's Lane. But no path or lane was ever dead straight and at the same time narrower than the winding by-ways that lead off from it. From the topography, Christian's way ought to correspond to the main road, but in allegorical terms it must not be either safe or broad, and what main road was ever so dangerously narrow, in places grassed over, and not used by the majority of people? Although the surrounding landscape is often realistically

The Broad and Narrow Way.

suggested, the way is unimaginable. Perhaps this is deliberate; perhaps Bunyan felt that a way to heaven which appeared like any kind of real road would seem too easy.

Shakespeare had referred to the "steep and thorny" way to heaven, contrasting it with the "primrose path of dalliance" or the "primrose path to the everlasting bonfire". Seventeenth-century writers of religious lyric poetry, likewise taking the difficulty of the way as the crucial thing, often see it as an overgrown path, or one with difficult stiles. Robert Herrick left a gay social life in London to become a village priest in Devon, and his poem *To His Everloving God* has a homely picture of heaven as a cluster of cottage roofs approached across country:

> Can I not come to Thee, my God, for these
> So very-many-meeting hindrances . . .
> Cleere Thou my paths, or shorten Thou my miles,
> Remove the barrs, or lift me o'er the stiles:
> Since rough the way is, help me when I call,
> And take me up; or els prevent the fall.
> I kenn my home; and it affords some ease,
> To see far off the smoaking Villages.

Thomas Traherne, a younger contemporary, gives a gloomier picture of a backsliding, or possibly a side-tracked, generation in his poem *Misapprehension*:

> But Man hath lost the ancient Way,
> That Road is gon into Decay;
> Brambles shut up the Path, and Briars tear
> Those few that pass by there.

This may have been one of the poems Edmund Blunden had in mind when he declared that Traherne's landscape was "won by experience", and he notes elsewhere that knowledge of footpaths is one of the marks of the true countryman. Blunden himself, in a poem called *April Byeway*, continued the tradition in the lines:

> Friend whom I never saw, yet dearest friend
> Be with me travelling on the byeway now"

John Drinkwater in *O Gracious One* prays in the same vein
that in times of adversity he will have God's company
"along thy footpaths". There is a suggestion, I think, in both
these poems that the humbler byeway and footpaths belong
to God and to good men.

In Tennyson the path of life image occurs, again as a footpath, but without religious or moral connotation. In his
great poem *In Memoriam*, a long threnody for the untimely
death of his friend Arthur Hallam, the path repeatedly
signifies the journey through life to death. The image strikes
the reader as fresh because it suggests a real picture of two
young men out walking together, a picture borne out even
within the poem by the lines:

> I climb the hill: from end to end
> Of all the landscape underneath,
> I find no place that does not breathe
> Some gracious memory of my friend;
> No gray old grange, or lonely fold,
> Or low morass and whispering reed,
> Or simple stile from mead to mead,
> Or sheepwalk up the windy wold.

The path of life they trod together was not particularly
difficult to begin with, although it becomes darker – in fact,
it is flowery: but the floweriness contains no hint of misspent youth:

> The path by which we twain did go,
> Which led by tracts that pleased us well,
> Through four sweet years arose and fell,
> From flower to flower, from snow to snow . . .

> But where the path we walked began
> To slant the fifth autumnal slope,
> As we descended following Hope,
> There sat the Shadow feared of man . . .

> I know that this was Life – the track
> Whereon with equal feet we fared.

It was Life, but it was also the wold and fen-land paths of Lincolnshire which he walked with Hallam in Cambridge vacations, when his friend stayed with the family at the Somersby Rectory. The verb "to fare" often occurs in contexts where the writer imagines life as a path. Tennyson was the first of a number of poets whose consciousness of landscape and whose habit of walking with friends gave them a mental image of life in terms of a footpath journey.

When Hardy went – a red-letter day for John Cowper – to visit the Powys household at Montacute, he was asked to add his name to the list in their ancient and sacred play-den. Humouring these grown-up children, and perhaps feeling a responsive chord in a sadder whimsicality of his own, he wrote: "Thomas Hardy, a Wayfarer". In terms of the game this was perfectly correct, since he was not one of the resident band or tribe. But, too, the image was an important one for him, and the figure of the wayfarer, often going across country by footpaths, is prominent in his novels and his poetry. The wanderer may be restlessly seeking what lies ahead, or he may be hounded from behind: both elements can be seen in the lives of Jude the Obscure and Tess. The full tragic power of the figure appears in Tess, whose first adventure is on a cart and vainly decked out, and whose subsequent declension from the pride of life is shown almost allegorically in her cross-country walk to Emminster and her penitential journey to Flintcombe-Ash with her beauty deliberately disfigured by a kerchief and clipped eyebrows. "Thus Tess walks on," wrote Hardy significantly, "a figure which is part of the landscape". Almost all his chief characters are at some time dwarfed and absorbed by the inhuman surrounding countryside: they merely pass through, and the very roads and paths they use, though made by human beings, outlast the individual.

The course of Tess's journey to Emminster is carefully plotted:

Keeping the Vale on her right, she steered steadily west-

ward; passing above the Hintocks, crossing at right-
angles the high-road from Sherton-Abbas to Casterbridge . . . Still following the elevated way she reached
Cross-in-Hand . . . Three miles further she cut across the
straight and deserted Roman road called Long-Ash
lane . . .

Fleeing vaguely from justice at the end, Clare and Tess use
footpaths for secrecy, "avoiding high roads, and following
obscure paths tending more or less northward".

In the poems the figure of the wayfarer, wanderer,
pilgrim or tramp appears constantly, and his journey is
often by footpath. Once Hardy's preoccupation becomes
plain it is possible – and I think right – to see a hint of the
figurative virtually wherever there is a journey, or a clue
word like "pilgrim" or "fare", or "track", "path", "way" or
"road", even in what is apparently a straightforwardly
descriptive passage. "By prowling paths" he is dogged by
his other self; he regrets not having joined "so true-footed a
farer" on his path; "paradise-paths" are the lovers' share;
"life's bare pathway", he tells us, "looms like a desert track
to me". *The Five Students*, a macabre version of a children's
dropping-out rhyme, describes a symbolic ride which continues as the seasons alter and the riders fail one by one.
"Paddock-path" and "track" as well as "high-road" make
up their course, and they have been hypothetically identified as his wife Emma, his sister Mary, the poet William
Barnes, his cousin Tryphena Sparks – all of whom pre-
deceased him – and himself. Even in his Introductory Note
to *Winter Words* Hardy speaks of "the track having been
adventured . . . before", picturing the course of his own
career as a journey by footpath. The lyric *If You Had Known*
describes:

> In turning home . . . the slow wet walk
> By crooked ways and over stiles of stone

and though brief it is not slight. It gains power from the pre-
vailing metaphor; yet the description reads literally, and the

The Stepping Stones: Myles Birket Foster.

poem would be less effective if it did not. We recognise a real path (a Cornish one, because of the stone stiles), crooked for historical and topographical reasons. But, too, it is maligantly crooked, and the stiles unfeelingly, coldly stone. The path is that of a tough life which a fragile rose could not withstand.

Even in his topographical prose Edward Thomas's paths often take on added bloom of visionary significance. As well as connecting real places, they have an air of leading to freedom, or knowledge, or beatitude. His small but precious corpus of poems seems to crystallise much of the experience suspended in the prose, and he gives to signpost, stile and path a mystical meaning beyond the thing itself.

"Green roads" and "many a road and track" lead into his recurrent death-forest. Then there is a path which leads nowhere, which children use, running along a bank above a road. He describes the path so that we see it clearly, "silvered . . . between the moss", and then tells us that it looks:

> As if it led on to some legendary
> Or fancied place where men have wished to go
> And stay; till, sudden, it ends where the wood ends.

So life ends? Or the pleasant fantasies of childhood? It is clear from this poem *The Path* that he can use "road" as Hardy did to mean any route. Because he liked to walk fast, paths easily became to him a metaphor for life's journey, because he used them for really getting somewhere. In *Over the Hills* he takes a specific experience:

> . . . the day I passed the horizon ridge
> To a new country, the path I had to find
> By half-gaps that were stiles once in the hedge . . .

and through it hints at ideas of opportunity, second chances, and nostalgia. Again, in Thomas's poem *It Was Upon*, he shows his especial skill in packing a number of related thoughts around the notion of a footpath journey:

> It was upon a July evening.
> At a stile I stood, looking along a path
> Over the country by a second Spring
> Drenched perfect green again. 'The lattermath
> Will be a fine one.' So the stranger said,
> A wandering man. Albeit I stood at rest,
> Flushed with desire I was. The earth outspread,
> Like meadows of the future, I possessed.

He had written in *The South Country*:

> It is hard to make anything like a truce between these two incompatible desires, the one for going on and on over the earth, the other that would settle for ever in one place as in a grave, and have nothing to do with change.

The word "grave" betrays his deep-seated fear of the settled life, but on that July evening the "two incompatible desires" seem temporarily reconciled: he seems able to possess the future without being himself the wandering man. Both in Hardy's poetry and in Thomas's the footpath may be the local familiar path of home, but it is more often the long "road" over the hills to an unknown destination. A late poem of Walter de la Mare's called *Solitude* uses the image in a way that recalls Thomas's death-forests:

> When the high road
> Forks into a by-road,
> And that drifts into a lane,
> And the lane breaks into a bridle-path,
> A chace forgotten
> Still as death,
> And green with the night's long rain . . .

This is characteristic of the way the poet transmutes the countryside into a fey and shadowy other-world, a tendency which explains why there are so few actual paths in the works of a poet who deals so extensively with English countryside and folk-lore.

> Life lies before thee, hardly stepped on yet,
> Like a green prairie, fresh, and full of flowers.
> Life lies before thee for experiment
> Until old age comes, whose sad eyes can trace
> A better path he missed, with fairer flowers . . .

So wrote W. H. Davies in *The Dreaming Boy*; he sees life as offering a choice of paths, and has a humanist's regret that not all can be tried. He who follows a quest, holy or unholy, must go where it leads; Browning's hero in *Childe Roland* obedient to his destiny goes the way he is directed to the Dark Tower:

> So, quiet as despair, I turned from him,
> That hateful cripple, out of his highway
> Into the path he pointed.

The Field Path: Paul Nash.

Richard Hurdis in an extended image in *The Village Curate* advocates the treading out of one's own path and eschewing the highroad:

> Let him speed who will,
> And fly like cannon-shot from post to post;
> I love to pause, and quit the public road,
> To gain a summit, take a view, or pluck
> An unknown blossom . . .
>   . . . In a path,

Peculiarly his own great Handel went . . .
                              . . . In a new course
Went Shakespeare.

In the context of the whole poem, which contains a good deal of the description and praise of footpaths, this image conveys a picture of a real path more clearly than is apparent from the quotation alone. In E. M. Forster's short story *The Other Side of the Hedge* the highroad of progress is seen as something to be shunned. The path through the meadows stands here too for freedom, thinking for oneself, and leaving the rat-race.

The by-paths of Dorset are both the real background of T. F. Powys's allegorical tales and at the same time the ways of the world; it is his intimate knowledge of these villages which gives them such power as microcosms. Bizarre and apparently unique occurrences on lanes and meadow-paths take on a universal symbolic significance; he studied human nature and the human predicament deeply and closely in a little place, and could thence illuminate it at large. A lane in his novel *Unclay* illustrates one of his methods of combining realistic description with obvious allegory:

> The lane began deceitfully. It looked pleasant enough at first, the beginning was grassy. One went along for a little admiring the may-blossoms, and then all at once fell into nettles, old boots, dock leaves, and broken bottles. If one struggled on, nothing better would come of it. There was no pleasure in going there. The lane narrowed; it became only brambles, long trailing brambles with sharp thorns. To struggle through these brought one into no fairy-land for at the end of the lane was but a slough made of cow-dung.

As Glen Cavaliero pointed out, he conveys "the feel, as much as the look, of stiles and paths and hedgerows". Here, the lane specifically exemplifies the process of disillusionment. On the whole, Powys's paths and lanes are merely paths of life because of his intensity, which makes the passions, affections and deaths of his characters universally significant. So confident is he in his method that he is able to play a little with it, again in *Unclay*, where as two characters approach each other on Folly Down he comments:

> If one walks upon a path – be it but a thyme-scented track over a down, or the tortuous and difficult way of a man's life – when another figure approaches from the opposite direction, the meeting always comes sooner than expected.

His short story called *Bottle's Path* must supply one of the latest references to the footpath-of-righteousness, and it seems to draw together various threads not only from this chapter, but from this book as a whole:

> Mr. Bottle's greatest interest in life, other than his religion, had always been footpaths, and it was said of him that, when he was a younger man, he knew every footpath in the county.
> Every sermon of Mr. Bottle's, that he preached in the chapel at Mockery where he lived, had some reference or other to a footpath, and he often used to say that it is upon one's own feet, walking in a lonely footway, and not upon a tarred road in an automobile, as Mr. Reed supposed, that one reaches God.

Mr. Bottle is one who knows and loves humble ways, and for him a footpath provides a metaphor for right living because it is simple, direct, and in touch with reality. The car symbolises pride and greed. Its noise, its speed, and the way it insulates its occupants from their neighbours and from the elements means to him a blocking of the ears against the still, small voice. The footpath nourishes the spirit.

Jean Ingelow, a contemporary of Tennyson's whose poetry has a number of footpath references, wrote a complex philosophical poem called *The Star's Monument*. In it the Poet, standing in a lane, sees a lyre-shaped shadow cast on the ground by two intertwined branches from the hedge. Her lines of comment might serve as an invocation for all those writers whose inspiration owes much to the paths, for in it the path is both inspiration and life:

> This lyre is cast across the dusty way,
> The common path that common men pursue;
> I crave like blessing for my shadowy lay,
> Life's trodden paths with beauty to renew.

Afterword

E DWARD Thomas's poem *Lob* pursues the spirit of Old England, an elusive, independent, and apparently indestructible earth-spirit, compounded, among other simples, of Puck and the common soldier. This spirit Thomas restlessly hunted up and down the by-ways; appropriately his first clue to its whereabouts appears in those splendidly truculent words:

> "Nobody can't stop 'ee. It's
> A footpath, right enough."

Already before the first world war writers like Ruskin and Thomas were lamenting the encroachments of suburbia. Today the landscape and rural life are greatly changed, and it seems likely that such inspiration as the paths now give tend to reflect man's increasingly unhappy relationship with the countryside. Hints of paths in recent poetry often lose themselves in tangles of introspection, like those in Robert Wells' *The Winter's Task*:

> If the land were less derelict, you might say
> You tamed the solitude through which you move,
> But you clear paths to lead yourself astray
> And endless wilderness their windings prove.

Insecurity, uncertainty and loss now seem to have infiltrated our thought and feeling so totally that we are scarcely surprised to find the paths leading nowhere but "endless wilderness". And, too, the rapid and sometimes wholesale diversion and extinguishment of old paths is one small symptom of the erosion of the countryside, a process which undermines the power to describe a felt and comprehended landscape as a stable background for more elusive human feelings. A poet who seems more at home in his landscape than most is Jeremy Hooker. He is helped perhaps by the fact that it is partly a seascape, which cannot be ravaged in so many ways. In *Pitts Deep* he realises that "No one will . . . cross the manorial path/Into oakwoods descending"

> Except, perhaps, two friends . . .
> Who walk in confessional mood
> Where forest ponies also go

but he conveys a sense of a continuity unbroken despite the diminished traffic of the path. This tone is in marked contrast to that of Peter Scupham's poem *Public Footpath To*, from which I quoted towards the end of Chapter 2. Here the landscape is hostile and unhelpful; adjectives like "cold", "sour", "lost", "chill", "forbidden" and "sullen" set the mood of alienation. In *Pitts Deep* the path is shared, with a friend and with the animals, and the landscape is benign, conducive to confidence. One poet believes he belongs on the path; the other does not.

Helen Thomas described movingly how she visited Ivor Gurney in mental hospital. She cheered and beguiled him from himself an hour or two by the blessed inspiration of some large-scale maps of his dear Gloucestershire, on which he could trace the paths he had known. He had rooted himself in a countryside and lived his best life through it. Edward Thomas himself was not without a certain educated, urbanised unease with the countryside. Nor did he ever belong to a particular place, which gives firm ground for feeling. But certain signposts Thomas erected, in

The Lickey, Worcestershire: Joseph E. Southall.

his brief life, and they pointed down quiet paths where there was time for thought. In the bustle with Eliot and Auden down main roads to the witty metropolis they were mainly ignored – the chronological table at the back of the book reflects the decline in rural writing. Now, in the seventies, writers and readers of poetry are searching out Thomas's paths once more.

Soon the eighties will be upon us. In George Orwell's still terrifying book *Nineteen Eighty-Four* the hero has a fantasy landscape that he calls the Golden Country. It is reached by a footpath through a beautiful wooded countryside, and he finds it exists in real life when a woman arranges to meet him there, out of range of the watchful telescreens. There they make love. The Golden Country is all that the Party and the spiritually impoverished urban existence is not.

1984 does not threaten in quite the way that Orwell presaged; but if we want the Golden Country to exist outside the imagination, we must keep the paths to it open.

Texts

THE texts of the poets given below are those to which the page numbers in the references refer. In the case of Barnes and Clare I have also suggested a useful selection.

Barnes, William: *The Poems* ed. Bernard Jones in 2 vols., Centaur Press, 1962

Barnes, William: *One Hundred Poems* with an essay by E. M. Forster, The Dorset Bookshop, 1971

Clare, John: *The Poems* ed. with an introduction by J. W. Tibble in 2 vols., J. M. Dent, 1935

Clare, John: *Selected Poems* ed. with an introduction by James Reeves. Poetry Bookshelf series, Heinemann, 1954 repr. 1976

Hardy, Thomas: *The Complete Poems* ed. James Gibson. The New Wessex edition, Macmillan, 1976

Thomas, Edward: *Collected Poems* Faber and Faber, 1936

Young, Andrew: *Complete Poems* arranged and introduced by Leonard Clark, Secker & Warburg, 1974

References

1. "Common Thoughts"   *Page*

Robert Southey: *English Eclogues* III, *The Ruined Cottage* 1.
   97ff., *Poems* Oxford, 1909, p. 417   1

Geoffrey Grigson: *Freedom of the Parish* London, 1954, p. 158   3

Sidney Webb: *The Story of the King's Highway*, vol. V of
   English Local Government London, 1906, p. 230ff.

John Hoole: quoted in the Life of John Scott prefacing his
   poems in *A Complete Edition of the Poets of Great Britain* vol.
   XI, London, 1795   4

John Scott: *Amoebean Eclogues* I, 1. 45ff., ibid.   5

Raymond Williams: *The Country and the City* London, 1973

Glen Cavaliero: *The Rural Tradition in the English Novel*
   London, 1977   7

John Clare: *Sketches in the Life of John Clare written by himself*
   published by Edmund Blunden, London, 1931, p. 45

John Clare: *The Flitting*, *Poems* vol. II, p. 252   8

Thomas Hardy: *Domicilium*, *Poems* p. 3   9

Edward Thomas: *A Literary Pilgrim in England* London, 1928,
   p. 146   10

Edward Thomas: *Richard Jefferies* repr. Faber, 1978, p. 44

Eleanor Farjeon: *Edward Thomas, the Last Four Years* London,
   1958, p. 134   11

Helen Thomas: *As It Was . . . World Without End* London,
   1935, p. 186   12

Edward Thomas: *A Diary in English Fields and Woods* in *The
   Woodland Life*

Page

Clare: *The Village Minstrel, Poems* vol. I, p. 156

A. W. B. Simpson: *Introduction to the History of Land Law* London, 1961, p. 244   28

Barnes: *The Cost of Improvement, Poems* p. 852

John Barrell: *The Idea of Landscape and the Sense of Place* Cambridge 1972, p. 94–6   29

Barnes: *The Leane, Poems* p. 308   30

Gerard Manley Hopkins: *Binsey Poplars, The Poems* 4th edn., London etc., 1967, p. 78

Mary Russell Mitford: *Violeting* and *The Cowslip Ball* in *Our Village* London etc., 1936, pp. 45 & 57

Sidney Webb: *English Local Government* vol. V, London, 1906, p. 230ff.   31

Jane Austen: *Emma* Ch. XII   32

Robert Wellbeloved: *On Highways* London, 1829, p. viiiff.

Arthur Conan Doyle: *The Hound of the Baskervilles* Ch. XI   33

Sidney Webb: *English Local Government* vol. V, London, 1906, p. 230ff.

Elizabeth Gaskell: *Mary Barton* Ch. I   34

Elizabeth Gaskell: *The Letters* ed. J. A. V. Chapple & A. Pollard, 1966, p. 68   35

Charles Dickens: *Bleak House* Ch. X; *The Old Curiosity Shop* Chs. LXXII & XXIV; *Hard Times* Book III, Ch. VI; *Little Dorritt* Book I, Ch. XXVIII; *Dombey & Son* Ch. XV   36ff

Clare: *Footpaths* I, *Poems* Vol II, p. 322   38

Rucksack, Journal of the Ramblers' Association, vol. 8, no. 8 Spring 1977 and subsequent issues   39

John Ruskin: *The Destruction of Footpaths* in *Arrows of the Chace*

John Ruskin: *Praeterita* I, II, 58

H. G. Wells: *Mr. Britling Sees It Through* Book III, Ch. I

Sheila Kaye-Smith: *Little England* Part I, Ch. I   40

Raymond Williams: *The Country and the City* London, 1973, Ch. IV   41

Herbert Read: *The Contrary Experience* London, 1963, Part IV, Ch. VII   42

Hardy: *The Return of the Native* Book III, Ch. II

Shakespeare: *King Lear* Act II, scene iv   44

Peter Scupham: *Prehistories* O.U.P., London, 1975

5. "Places of No Good Character"

	Page
Elizabeth Gaskell: *Cranford* Ch. X	87
Anthony Trollope: *The Last Chronicle of Barset* vol. I, Ch. XXXV	
Lucy Baxter: *The Life of William Barnes* London, 1887, p. 305	
Barnes: *Eclogue: A Ghost, Poems* p. 184–6	88
Mary Webb: *Precious Bane* Book I, Ch. IV	
Thomas Heywood: *The Witches of Lancashire* Act II, scene i	
Robert Graves: *The Two Witches, Collected Poems* London, 1975, p. 220	89
Walter de la Mare: *Berries, The Complete Poems* London, 1969, p. 154	
Eleanor Farjeon: *Edward Thomas, the Last Four Years* London, 1958, pp. 5, 10	
Eleanor Farjeon: *Eleanor Farjeon's Book* London, 1960, p. 7ff.	90
Barnes: *The Girt Wold House o' Mossy Stone, Poems* p. 224	
Hardy: *Yuletide in a Younger World, Poems* p. 861	91
Barnes: *Our Father's Works, Poems* p. 270	
Hardy: *The Head Above the Fog, Poems* p. 520	
J. O. Bailey: *The Poetry of Thomas Hardy* Chapel Hill, 1970, p. 235	92
Hardy: *Old Excursions, Poems* p. 520; *Her Immortality, Poems* p. 55; *Paying Calls, Poems* p. 506; *My Spirit Will Not Haunt the Mound, Poems* p. 318	
Vernon Watkins: *The Ballad of the Outer Dark* London, 1979	94
Shakespeare: *The Merry Wives of Windsor* Act III, scene i	
Richard Brinsley Sheridan: *The Rivals* Act V, scene iii	
Dickens: *Sketches by Boz, Tales* Ch. 8; *Pickwick Papers* Ch. II	
Shakespeare: *King Lear* Act IV, scene i; *The Winter's Tale* Act IV, scene ii	95
Thomas Heywood: *A Maydenhead Well Lost* Act II, scene i	96
Hardy: *Desperate Remedies* Ch. XX	
George Meredith: *The Egoist* Ch. XXVI	97
George Eliot: *The Mill on the Floss* Book II. Ch. II; *Adam Bede* Chs. XXXV & XXXVII	
John Drinkwater: *The Gypsy, Poems for a Child*, London, etc., n.d.	98
Llewelyn Powys: *Somerset & Dorset Essays* London, 1957, p. 41–2	
Hardy: *Winter Night in Woodland, Poems* p. 734	99

	Page
J. C. Powys: *Autobiography* Ch. VII	111
Llewelyn Powys: *A Baker's Dozen* London, 1941, p. 43	112
J. C. Powys: *Wolf Solent* Ch. II; *Autobiography* Ch. XII	

7. "Sounds and Scents and Seeings"

Edmund Blunden: *A Pastoral, The Poems* London, 1930, p. 123	116
William Collins: *Ode to Evening, The Poems* Boston etc., 1898, p. 53	
Edmund Blunden: *Sussex* repr. In *Edmund Blunden, A Selection* ed. K. Hopkins, London, 1950, p. 26	117
Clare: *Wild Bees, Poems* vol. II, p. 18	
Jefferies: *The Gamekeeper at Home* Ch. III; *The Amateur Poacher* Ch. VI	
Barnes: esp. *Lewth, Poems* p. 504	
Francis Kilvert: Diary 16 July 1873 (Penguin selection p. 235)	118
Jefferies: *Out of Doors in February* in *The Open Air*	119
Clare: *Recollections after an Evening Walk, Poems* vol. I, p. 76	
Clare: *Recollections after a Ramble, Poems* vol. I, p. 183	
Barnes: *Soft Sounds, Poems* p. 896	
William Cobbett: *Rural Rides*, 11 November, 1822	
Jefferies: *The Amateur Poacher* Ch. VI	
Leigh Hunt: *A Rustic Walk & Dinner* 11. 350–1, *The Poetical Works* Oxford etc., 1923, p. 277	120
Constance Holme: *The Lonely Plough* Ch. II	
Jefferies: *Green Ferne Farm* Ch. I	
Mary Russell Mitford: *Frost & Thaw* in *Our Village* London, 1936, p. 22	
Clare: *The Field Path, Poems* vol. II, p. 330	121
Jefferies: *Vignettes from Nature* II in *The Hills & the Vale*	
Clare: *The Days of April, Poems* vol. II, p. 406	
Jefferies: *Walks in the Wheatfields* in *Field & Hedgerow; The Amateur Poacher* Ch. VI	122
Clare: *The Wheat Ripening, Poems* vol. I, p. 526	123
Mary Russell Mitford: *The Young Gypsy* in *Our Village* London, 1936, p. 181	
J. C. Powys: *Maiden Castle* Ch. III	

Page

Clare: *Field Thoughts, Poems* vol. II, p. 307; *Summer Morning, Poems* vol. 1, p. 66   135f
John Keats: *'I Stood Tip-Toe Upon a Little Hill', The Poetical Works* Oxford, 1958, p. 5   136
Andrew Young: *Steyning, Poems* p. 348
Ivor Gurney: *Walking Song, Poems* London, 1973, p. 50; *The Escape*, ibid., p. 79

8. "Untrodden Ways"

Washington Irving: *Rural Life in England* in *The Sketch Book*   137
W. J. Keith: *The Rural Tradition*, Toronto etc., 1975
Raymond Williams: *The Country & the City* London, 1973, Ch. XXI
J. C. Powys: *Wood & Stone* Chs. XIII, VI; *Rodmoor* Ch. VII; *Wolf Solent* Ch. VII   138f
Tennyson: *The Gardener's Daughter, The Poems* ed. C. Ricks, London, 1969, p. 513   139
William Browne: *Britannia's Pastorals* Book I, song 2, *The Poems*, London, 1894, p. 47
Victoria Sackville-West: *The Land, Winter* London, 1926   140
Jefferies: *The Dewy Morn* Ch. XXII
Edward Thomas: *Horae Solitariae* Ch. XV
D. H. Lawrence: *Lady Chatterley's Lover* Ch. V; *Sons & Lovers* Ch. VI   141f
W. F. Hudson: *Afoot in England* Ch. XXIII   144
Henry Thoreau: *Walking and the Wild* in *The Footpath Way* ed. H. Belloc, 1911
Edward Thomas: *The South Country* Ch. III   145
Grant Allen: *The British Barbarians* Ch. IV
Francis Brett Young: *Mr. Lucton's Freedom* Part II, Ch. VI   146
E. M. Forster: *Howards End* Ch. XIV
Clare: *Trespass, Poems* vol. II, p. 373   147
D. H. Lawrence: *The White Peacock* Part II, Ch. I
Anthony Trollope: *Barchester Towers* Ch. XXII   148
Anthony Trollope: *The Last Chronicle of Barset* vol. I, Ch. XXVIII
Andrew Young: *Private, Poems* p. 342   149f

References · 183

Chronological Table

This list is highly selective and idiosyncratic. It aims to give an impressionistic outline of who was writing when, and not a complete bibliographical record. In the interests of brevity and clarity I omit many writers and works mentioned in the text, including only those which for various reasons seem to me to provide significant comparisons.

1803 Bloomfield: *The Farmer's Boy* and *Rural Tales*
1810 Wordsworth: *Guide to the Lakes*
1813 Jane Austen: *Pride and Prejudice*
1816 Jane Austen: *Emma*
1818 Jane Austen: *Persuasion*
1819 Washington Irving: *The Sketch Book*
1820 Clare: *Poems Descriptive of Rural Life and Scenery*
1821 Clare: *The Village Minstrel*
1824 Mitford: *Our Village* – first volume
1827 Clare: *The Shepherd's Calendar*
1829 Cobbett: *Rural Rides*
1832 Mitford: *Our Village* – last volume
1835 Clare: *The Rural Muse*
1836 Dickens: *Sketches by Boz* and *Pickwick*
1838 Howitt: *The Rural Life of England*
1844 Barnes: *Poems of Rural Life in the Dorset Dialect*
1848 Gaskell: *Mary Barton*
1850 Tennyson: *In Memoriam*
1852 Dickens: *Bleak House*

1853 Arnold: *Poems* inc. *The Scholar Gipsy*; Gaskell: *Cranford*
1854 Dickens: *Hard Times*
1857 Trollope: *Barchester Towers*
1859 Barnes: *Hwomely Rhymes*; George Eliot: *Adam Bede*
1860 George Eliot: *The Mill on the Floss*
1861 George Eliot: *Silas Marner*
1862 Barnes: *Poems of Rural Life*, 3rd collection
1863 Hawthorne: *Our Old Home*; Jean Ingelow: *Poems*
1864 Burritt: *London to John o'Groats*
1865 Burritt: *London to Land's End*
1866 George Eliot: *Felix Holt*
1870 Francis Kilvert's Diary begins
1871 Hardy: *Desperate Remedies*
1872 Hardy: *Under the Greenwood Tree*
1874 Hardy: *Far from the Madding Crowd*
1878 Hardy: *The Return of the Native*; Jefferies: *The Gamekeeper at Home*
1879 Jefferies: *Wild Life in a Southern County* and *The Amateur Poacher*; Meredith: *The Egoist*
1880 Jefferies: *Green Ferne Farm* and *Hodge and his Masters*; Hardy: *The Trumpet Major*
1883 Jefferies: *Nature Near London*
1884 Jefferies: *The Dewy Morn* and *The Life of the Fields*
1885 Jefferies: *The Open Air*
1886 Hardy: *The Mayor of Casterbridge*; Ruskin: *Praeterita*
1887 Hardy: *The Woodlanders*; Jefferies: *Amaryllis at the Fair*
1888 Hardy: *Wessex Tales*
1891 Hardy: *Tess of the d'Urbervilles*
1895 Grant Allen: *The British Barbarians*
1896 Hardy: *Jude the Obscure*
1897 Edward Thomas: *The Woodland Life*
1898 Hardy: *Wessex Poems*; E. Thomas: *Horae Solitariae*
1902 Conan Doyle: *The Hound of the Baskervilles*; Hardy: *Poems of the Past and Present*
1905 Kipling: *An Habitation Enforced*
1906 S. Webb: *The Story of the King's Highway*
1907 E. M. Forster: *The Longest Journey*
1908 E. M. Forster: *A Room with a View*
1909 E. Thomas: *The South Country* and *Richard Jefferies*; Hudson: *Afoot in England*; Hardy: *Time's Laughingstocks*

1910   E. M. Forster: *Howard's End*; Wells: *The History of Mr. Polly*
1911   D. H. Lawrence: *The White Peacock*
1913   de la Mare: *Peacock Pie*; D. H. Lawrence: *Sons and Lovers*; Trevelyan: *Walking*
1914   Constance Holme: *The Lonely Plough*
1915   J. C. Powys: *Wood and Stone*; D. H. Lawrence: *The Rainbow*
1916   W. H. Davies: *Collected Poems* (first collection)
1917   E. Thomas: *Poems*
1918   E. Thomas: *Last Poems*
1919   V. Woolf: *Night and Day*
1920   D. H. Lawrence: *Women in Love*
1922   Hardy: *Late Lyrics*
1924   Mary Webb: *Precious Bane*
1925   Watkins: *The Old Straight Track*; Blunden: *English Poems* (first collection)
1926   H. Thomas: *As It Was*
1928   D. H. Lawrence: *Lady Chatterley's Lover*; Hardy: *Winter Words*
1929   J. C. Powys: *Wolf Solent*
1930   Beatrix Potter: *The Tale of Little Pig Robinson*
1931   T. F. Powys: *Unclay*
1932   J. C. Powys: *A Glastonbury Romance*
1933   T. H. White: *Farewell Victoria*
1934   J. C. Powys: *Weymouth Sands* and *Autobiography*
1935   L. Powys: *Dorset Essays*
1936   J. C. Powys: *Maiden Castle*; A. Young: *Collected Poems* (first collection)
1939   Flora Thompson: *Lark Rise*
1940   Brett Young: *Mr. Lucton's Freedom*; W. Plomer: *Selected Poems*
1946   T. F. Powys: *Bottle's Path and other stories*
1948   F. Thompson: *Still Glides the Stream*
1950   A. Uttley: *The Cobbler's Shop*
1952   G. Grigson: *Freedom of the Parish*
1958   E. Farjeon: *Edward Thomas, the last Four Years*
1975   Peter Scupham: *Prehistories*
1978   D. Sharp: *Walking in the Countryside*; J. Hooker: *Solent Shore*

Index of Authors
and Artists Cited